Managing the Generation Mix: Second Edition

From Urgency to Opportunity

*Carolyn A. Martin, Ph.D.
and Bruce Tulgan*

HRD PRESS, INC.
Amherst, Massachusetts

Cover design by Eileen Klockars
Editorial services by Mary George
Production services by Anctil Virtual Office

In memory of John Martin, a member of the
Greatest Generation, whose life of
quiet bravery inspired his Boomer children
to succeed far beyond his fondest dreams.

And to Victoria D. Martin, the
energetic eightysomething who continues
to astonish those Boomers with
her strength and persistence.

Table of Contents

Acknowledgments vii

*Prequel: What You Need to Know
Before You Read This Book* xi

Introduction to the Second Edition xix

PART ONE: **Who's in Your Generation Mix Today?**
What You Can Expect 1

Chapter 1. The Schwarzkopf Generation:
Take Charge and Do What's Right 3

Chapter 2. Baby Boomers:
Trendsetters to the End 21

Chapter 3. Generation X:
What's the Deal Today? 39

Chapter 4. Generation Y: We're Here Today! 55

Chapter 5. Bridging the Generational
(Mis)Understanding Gap 81

PART TWO: **What Does It Take to Become a Great Gen Mix Manager?**
             What You Can Expect............................. 95

Chapter 6.   Focus: It's All About the Work 97

Chapter 7.   Communicate Just-in-Time,
             All the Time 113

Chapter 8.   Customize! Customize! Customize! 141

PART THREE: **From Retirees to Teens: Four Opportunities for the Taking**
             What You Can Expect............................. 161

Chapter 9.   Turning Gray to Gold: How to Mine
             the Riches in Seasoned Talent 163

Chapter 10. Heading Off the Midlevel
             Leadership Crisis: Who's
             Going to Take Charge? 181

Chapter 11. Managing Your Parents—
             or Grandparents: You're in
             Good Company 201

Chapter 12. Teaching Teens How to Serve
             Your Customers: How Well Are
             You Doing?.. 219

Conclusion: What You Need to Know
             After You Read This Book 229

Recommended Resources.. 231

Acknowledgments

AS ALWAYS, we are grateful to the thousands of people who, over the years, have shared their workplace experiences with us, giving voice and vitality to our ongoing research at RainmakerThinking, Inc. Topping the list for this project are the audiences in our Managing the Generation Mix workshops who, over the past five years, have taught us so many invaluable lessons. They were not only proud of their own generation, but open to the possibility that other generations could actually teach them something.

To the Schwarzkopfers we've met along the way, we are in awe of your wisdom and vitality, and we thank you for your willingness to share your knowledge with those who follow in your footsteps. The workplace needs you in ways it is only beginning to understand.

To the Boomers, you've done it again: You're in the right place at the right time in history. We thank you for creating new and graceful ways to age and retire. Let the good times keep on rolling!

To the Gen Xers: You've arrived and showed everyone you were not slackers after all! We thank you for taking the responsibility of becoming our next generation of leaders. We have great faith that you will do it in new and exciting ways.

To the Gen Yers: We thank you for your honesty, energy, talent, and "can-do" attitude. We can't wait to see how life unfolds for you. You just may be the next "Greatest Generation."

On the home front, we are particularly grateful to Jeff Coombs, our friend and business partner, who keeps RainmakerThinking running smoothly while we hop airplanes, meet great people, and write books. We wouldn't have a business without you, Jeff.

Special thanks to our friend and publisher, Bob Carkhuff, and his staff at HRD Press. Bob has continuously supported our work since the early days. The partnership we maintain with HRD Press is critical to our ability to reach inside organizations of every shape and size and make them even better than they already are. We are especially grateful to Mary George for her consistently excellent editing (she makes us better writers with every pocket guide) and to Eileen Klockars for her eye-catching cover designs.

As co-authors, we also have our respective debts of gratitude to express.

From Carolyn: Thank you to my Schwarzkopfer friends and colleagues Wilda Parks, Betty McQuilken, and Paul and Charlotte Enberg, who helped me shed preconceived notions about this talented, dedicated, often outrageous cohort; to Woodstockers Carol Cate, Cindy Knutson, Valerie Murtzl, Mike Peterson, Don Westing, and Kim Woodward, who epitomize what it means to be expert leaders and managers; to Young Boomers Jane P. Ellis, Jennie Messmer, and Millie Thomas, who are strong voices for their emerging cohort; to Gen Xers and Gen Yers Sarah

Galbraith, Isis Radcliffe, Matt Smith, and Mark Yorsaner, who continue to enlighten us about the best of their generations; and to my best friend, Kathy Richard, a practical Young Boomer who challenges my Woodstocker idealism every day.

From Bruce: Thank you from the bottom of my heart to my wise family and friends, who are the center of my universe. As always, I reserve my deepest thanks for my wife, the brilliant Dr. Debby Applegate.

Prequel: What You Need to Know Before You Read This Book

THE FOLLOWING IS EXCERPTED in large part from "Trends Point to a Dramatic Generational Shift in the Future Workforce," an article by Bruce Tulgan that originally appeared in Employee Relations Today *(Wiley: Winter 2004, Volume 30, Issue 4, pp. 23–31).*

The Generational Shift

On Labor Day 1993, I started conducting in-depth interviews with employees about work attitudes. At first, I was investigating the generation gap between older employees and the new Generation X (born 1965 to 1977), employees who were then entering the workforce.

When they first appeared in the workplace, Generation Xers were widely viewed as being less loyal than previous generations, and unwilling to pay their dues and climb the proverbial ladder. They didn't trust large institutions to make good on promises about long-term rewards, and so, for short-term sacrifices, they demanded immediate gratification.

Xers also turned away from the traditional career path and its norms of success, acting like free agents. They were always asking, "What's the deal around here? What do you want from me today? What do I get in return today?"

At first, older generations viewed this as a youthful aberration. "If we wait these kids out, everything will be okay," they assured one another. "Xers will outgrow this nonsense and grow into 'real adults' who will make 'real adult' commitments to our organization."

But then, the tech boom turned into the dot.com craze and it seemed like Generation Xers were taking over the world. All of a sudden, they were touted as super-workers with magical business models, making fortunes without ever having services or products, much less customers. They suddenly became the most sought-after workforce in the heady days of the late 1990s, when unemployment stood at record lows, talent wars raged in every industry, never-ending streams of good news blanketed business pages, record numbers of new businesses were started, job creation was at record highs, and job hopping was common.

And with these Gen X super-workers came a free agent mindset that boldly proclaimed, "Jobs may come and jobs may go, but my career belongs to me. So, what's the deal around here today?"

This free agency attitude, however, didn't come out of a booming economy alone. Remember, the 90s started out with a downsizing, restructuring, and reengineering revolution that attacked fundamental notions about long-term job security. Driven by the great forces of history—technology and globalization—organizations reached a new stage of global interconnection, high speed, and complexity. The worldwide business environment became one of high risk, erratic markets, and unpredictable resource needs. In order to adjust, organizations of all sizes had to become more lean and flexible. Even as robust numbers of new jobs were created during the boom, more than a million were lost every year.

By the end of the 90s, few employees of any age believed that paying dues and climbing a corporate ladder would be rewarded with long-term job security and financial payoffs. As thousands of Baby Boomers were let go from jobs they held for 15 to 20 years, they finally understood what Generation X had known from day one: Job security was a myth. And workers of every generation finally laid that myth to rest six feet under.

Many analysts and older managers in the 90s had simply gotten it wrong: the "Gen X" employee attitude wasn't a youthful aberration. It was a vanguard response to the first stages of transformation in the workplace. It was an accident of history. Largely unaware of the historic changes underway, Xers were responding naturally to a workplace without the promise of job security.

Their workplace revolution turned out to be very real, but it was never about casual dress, desk-massages, astronomical pay, foosball tables, and pizza. It was about employees taking care of themselves and their families; it was about employees leveraging their talents, skills, time, and energy; it was about employees trying to get what they could in return from their employers today, since there was no assurance that any job would still exist tomorrow.

The Generational Shift Today

At the writing of this book, we at RainmakerThinking are still conducting research on the front lines of the workplace. What are we finding today? The workplace revolution precipitated by globalization and technology has accelerated and become more pervasive. Without credible long-term promises from employers, employees of all ages and at all levels no longer labor quietly and obediently. Rather, most realize that they are "free agents" because they have no other choice. It's every person for him- and herself. When organizations no longer feel a responsibility toward their workers, self-responsibility becomes the rallying cry of the workforce. Gen Xers were the first to utter that cry now heard around America—and around the world.

In just about every organization in just about every industry, managers are under increasing pressure from senior executives to deliver on more demanding marching orders: "Get more work and better work out of fewer employees using fewer resources."

With that directive in one hand and the needs, demands, and expectations of their employees in the other, managers find that managing and motivating employees now requires more time and skill than ever before. The most effective of them have learned to rely on the power of interpersonal communication skills by engaging direct reports in ongoing coaching dialogues about performance standards, goals, and deadlines.

They've learned how to maximize their power by doing more for people who do more for them. They bend over backwards to gain control of discretionary resources and then use those resources as day-to-day bargaining chips to

---

**Want to Learn More
About the Workplace Revolution?**

A free executive summary of this topic, based on our
extensive workplace research, is now available online.
Simply visit http://rainmakerthinking.com and click
at our White Papers link; or directly link on at
http://rainmakerthinking.com/rschrpts.htm.

---

drive high performance. Finally, these managers tend to be
extremely rigorous about holding employees accountable
on a daily basis: setting expectations clearly, correcting
performance problems immediately, and quickly removing
low performers from the workplace.

As a result, the most successful managers today have
redefined the manager-employee relationship to achieve
one major goal: getting the best results for the organization
while addressing the needs and demands of individual
contributors.

The Generational Shift Continues

The workplace revolution of the last decade has been
profound, but now there are powerful demographic forces
underway that will cement the Generational Shift once and
for all:

- First, those of the Schwarzkopf Generation (born before
  1946) are gradually exiting the workforce and taking with
  them decades of wisdom, knowledge, and expertise.

Researchers predict that in 2006 two experienced workers will leave the workforce for every one inexperienced worker who enters.

- Second, Baby Boomers (born 1946 to 1964) are becoming the aging workforce; every day eight to 10 thousand Baby Boomers turn 55. In fact, the U.S. Department of Labor projects that over the next eight years the over-55 workforce will grow by 49.3 percent.

- Third, the prime-age workforce—those 35- to 45-year-olds who are the prime candidates for leadership positions—will be made up increasingly of Generation X (born 1965 to 1977), followed closely by Generation Y (born 1978 to 1989).

No matter how effective organizations become at retaining older workers by offering them flexible roles, Generation X and Generation Y will soon become the dominant players in the workplace. As they do, they will usher out the last vestiges of the old-fashioned workplace values and norms and finish the workplace revolution.

Ironically, these younger generations will be supported by huge cadres of aging workers (often with significant power in organizations) who will need and demand more flexible work conditions, thus pushing the "free agent" agenda in their own ways for their own reasons. And then, of course, the next new generation of younger workers, with no attachment at all to the old-fashioned career path and work patterns, will emerge.

What Will These Changes Mean?

For the foreseeable future, as the revolution in workplace values and norms continues, pressure will increase on managers and employees alike. Managers will have to discard traditional notions of authority, rules, and red tape, and become more highly engaged in one-on-one coaching and negotiating with employees. They will have to abandon the one-size-fits-all approach to employer-employee relations in order to drive productivity, quality, and innovation. And they will have to become very astute at hiring the best person—regardless of age—for every role at every level, and then become very disciplined at managing every person aggressively to reach higher levels of productivity.

The most successful workers will have to accept the fact that their career belongs to them. They will have to take responsibility for their own success and fend for themselves as best they can. They will have to focus on learning marketable skills, building relationships with decision makers, and selling their way into career opportunities that help them define success in their own terms.

Introduction to the Second Edition

WHEN *MANAGING THE GENERATION MIX* was first published in 2002, the topic of generational diversity had been our focus for nearly a decade and was working itself onto the radar screens of most business leaders. Organizations were just figuring out how to recruit Generation X into their ranks when a new group of employees, popularly known as Generation Y, came pounding on their doors. Suddenly, they had two cohorts of young talent clashing, not only with older employers but with each other, over every workplace issue imaginable, from scheduling, dress codes, and incentives to respect for authority, work ethic, and management styles. And few organizations knew what to do about it.

Since 2002, that conflict has increased as millions of Gen Yers—full of attitude and expectation—have streamed into the workplace and millions of older workers—full of knowledge and experience—have streamed out. People who were initially skeptical about the topic of generational diversity came to realize its importance. Not just age, but generational cohort, was becoming another lens—like those of gender, race, religion, and culture—through which to look at people's workplace experiences and needs. Generational difference is a powerful framework for defining what binds certain groups together and what drives other groups absolutely crazy. If you have parents or grandparents who grew up during the Great Depression, siblings who witnessed the turbulent 60s and Watergate, or teenagers who zip effortlessly around the Internet, you know all about those intergenerational, crazy-making clashes at home.

In today's workplace, generational diversity is still driving some people to distraction. What do we hear in our seminars every day? Here are a few examples:

- "Gen Yers have an unrealistic sense of entitlement when they come to work. They want higher-ranking positions than their experience and education dictate. They may be great Little Leaguers, but they have no idea what it means to play in the Big Leagues."

- "Baby Boomers think they're great change leaders but they're still stuck in the status quo. They don't know how to be flexible."

- "Gen Xers don't want to follow our management career path. They aren't willing to commit the time. All they want to do is leave at 6 p.m. to have dinner with their family."

- "Older generations don't work as smart as we younger people do. They don't want to learn technology and they tell us to slow down. If we can get results in six hours, why do we have to hang around for eight?"

Sound familiar?

In every conceivable industry, managers like you tell us they are still tackling age-related challenges every day. Some are having difficulty with Gen-Y new hires who inform them about 17 things wrong with their organization—even before orientation. Others are finding it difficult to manage people old enough to be their parents—or grandparents. Still others are at a loss about how to adjust their communication style to fit people who prefer instant messaging, email, face-to-face conversations—or no communication at all.

In this era of accelerated change and fierce competition, we felt an urgency to revisit the insights, skills, and best practices we recommended to managers of multigenerational teams in the first edition of this pocket guide. We wanted to determine the answers to four major questions:

1. What has changed for each generation in terms of their needs and expectations today?

2. Which of our recommendations to managers of multigenerational teams still hold true today?

3. What new strategies, tactics, and best practices will help these managers become even more effective as the workplace revolution accelerates?

4. What opportunities must managers seize today to attract, retain, and motivate the best talent of all generations given the dramatic demographics changes in the workforce we call the Generational Shift?

How dramatic are those changes? Consider the following:

Generations X and Y
- In 2005, the scale tipped in the workplace once and for all. Together, Generation X and Generation Y now make up the majority of the workforce.

Estimated U.S. Civilian Non-Institutional Workforce by Generation

2006 RainmakerThinking Analysis

Cohort (Birth Years)	Percentage
Generation Y (1978–89)	22.0%
Generation X (1965–77)	29.5%
Baby Boomers (1946–64)	41.5%
Schwarzkopf Generation (before 1946)	7.0%

- While the percentage of Gen Xers in the workforce has remained constant since 2001 at 29.5 percent, that of Gen Yers has naturally increased, with Generation Y becoming the fastest-growing segment.

- Between now and 2011, roughly 10 million more Gen Yers will join the workforce, not including immigrant members. By 2011, Generation Y will outnumber Generation X. And by then the next "young generation" will be nipping at the heels of Generation Y.

Baby Boomers
- In the United States alone, approximately 330 Woodstockers (first-wave Boomers) turn 60 every hour! That's an additional 7,920 sixtysomethings every day every year for the next decade.

- Even as Boomers remain dominant players in many organizations, millions have left organizations and millions more will leave, long before traditional retirement age.

- Some Boomers have simply cashed out and are laughing all the way to the golf course. But others—downsized, restructured, and reengineered out of jobs—have become free agents, leveraging their skills as temps, consultants, independent contractors, or freelancers. Still others have followed their entrepreneurial impulses and started their own businesses. Some are taking early retirement, whether they can afford it or not, and finding new workplaces that endorse their desire for flexibility. Many are redefining aging and retirement in ways that will challenge organizations for the next decade.

The Senior Generation ("Schwarzkopfers")
- In the United States alone, more than one million Americans 75 years of age or older are still active in the workforce. Millions more are between the ages of 65 and 74, collectively representing a vast store of skills, knowledge, wisdom, institutional memory, relationships, and the last vestiges of the old-fashioned work ethic.

- Despite the hardiness of some members, this cohort will continue streaming out of the workforce and virtually disappear from the workplace by 2011.

Across the Generations
- Again, roughly two experienced workers currently leave the workforce for every one inexperienced worker who enters it.

- By 2011 the number of prime-age workers—
the 35- to 45-year-olds from whom organizations
draw the majority of their midlevel managers—will
decrease by more than 10 percent. That will leave
organizations with a shrinking pool of leadership
candidates.

Given these statistics and projections, the pressure is on
every manager to seize every opportunity to increase
management effectiveness with the multigenerational
workforce. Talent is still the name of the game. Why?
Numbers. Because of slow population growth between
1966 and 1985, there aren't enough Gen Xers and Gen
Yers to take the place of the members of older generations
who will retire during the next five years. Every skilled
worker of every age will be needed in every successful
enterprise.

Today, the opportunity to be on the bleeding edge of
organizations who maximize the talents, skills, experience,
and wisdom of every age group is there for the taking.
"You're too young" or "You're too old" are moot points and
need to be eliminated immediately from your hiring criteria.
Who cares if someone is 19 or 59? Can they do the work
that needs to get done today? Can they learn the skills
necessary to become up-to-date knowledge workers who
consistently add value to the workplace and to their own
lives? Do they have the willingness to leverage their talents
and expertise in collaborative and innovative efforts?

A Word on Generational Definitions: Second Edition Update

Many experts still agree there are four distinct generational cohorts in today's workplace—and still disagree on nomenclature and exact parameters. Some call the oldest workers Veterans, Matures, or Traditionals, and set their birth years at any time before 1943. Others label them "the Silent Generation," with birth years between 1925 and 1942. We now call them the Schwarzkopf Generation—with all due respect to the General—and set their birth dates before 1946.

Some say the Baby Boom began in 1943 with the "Victory Children"; others start it in 1946, after the end of World War II. We now divide this huge generation into two distinct waves:

- The Woodstock Generation, born 1946 to 1953
- The Young Boomers, born 1954 to 1964

Some claim that Generation Xers were born between 1961 and 1983, with Generation Yers—or "Millennials," "Nexters," or "Echo Boomers"—born between 1982 and 2002. We narrow the gap, setting the birth years for Xers at 1965 to 1977, and those for Yers at 1978 to 1989.

Of course, every day we still meet people who rebel at being put into any age-group category at all. "I can't identify with Generation X," explains a thirtysomething. "I was raised by my grandparents on a farm. My work ethic and values are more Veteran than X." A sixtysomething accuses us of outrageous stereotyping by putting people into age boxes. A fiftysomething says coworkers call him "Boom-X" because of his free agency mindset.

Perhaps the truth is that generations are in the eye of the age holder, viewed from as many different perspectives as there are unique individuals in the world. Certainly we believe that stereotyping people according to age is as misguided and counterproductive as stereotyping them according to gender, race, culture, or religion. Still, our research since the early 1990s, backed by our extensive work with people in hundreds of organizations, tells us that it is highly instructive to look at the trends in attitudes and behavior that define generational identities. These trends, we know, are directly tied to growing up and coming of age during the same historical period amidst the same key historical influences. That's what it means to be part of a generational cohort. For managers, it is vitally important to understand the power in those cohorts and the particular strengths that each brings to the workplace.

What You Can Expect

The second edition of *Managing the Generation Mix* is designed to heighten your sense of urgency about generational diversity in the workplace so that you will seize every opportunity to turn that diversity into one of your biggest assets. It will help you maximize the strengths of your age-diverse team members by offering practical answers to questions that managers across the country ask us every day:

- What is the "generation mix" today? What coming-of-age experiences have shaped each cohort's workplace attitudes, values, and perspectives? How have those attitudes, values and perspectives changed as each generation has moved from the workplace of the past into that of the present?

- How do you bridge the understanding gap among generations to clear obstacles to more productive relationships?

- How do you leverage everyone's unique talents so all team members focus on the only finish line that matters: the highest-quality results achieved in record time by the highest-quality talent?

- In addition to all the management skills you've already mastered, what other core competencies and best practices will help you more effectively lead a collaborative Gen Mix team?

- What urgent multigenerational challenges, precipitated by the Generational Shift, demand your immediate attention? What opportunities must you seize to meet them head-on?

In addition to answering these questions, we've also included the most popular and effective team exercises we facilitate during our Managing the Generation Mix workshops. Most of these interactive activities can be completed within the time frame of a typical staff meeting. They will give people of all ages the opportunity to become better contributors to and creators of your multigenerational team.

Remember: Generational Issues Are Business Issues

Generational issues are not simply about being part of or identifying with a particular cohort. Generational issues also mirror the critical business issues organizations face as every employee of every age group joins the workplace revolution. Age-related issues are not simply matters of "young versus old." Rather, they are matters of adapting to and embracing the historic paradigm shifts that have redefined the employer-employee relationship and the meaning of loyalty, working life, and career.

Your challenge as a Gen Mix manager is to help your team make the transition from the workplace of the past to that of the future more quickly, creatively, and collaboratively. Your major goal is to steer your multigenerational team members off the rigid course of "business as usual" into an open field of innovation, productivity, and shared learning. This book will help you reach that goal by raising your own generational awareness and understanding, and steering you onto a course of greater management competency. We're betting that you will feel the urgency in that goal and have the wisdom to seize every opportunity to achieve it.

> *How generationally savvy are you?*
> *To find out, test your GENERATIONAL I.Q.*

Generational I.Q. Test: *Who Said It?*

Directions: Are you generationally savvy? Find out by identifying the generation that each of the following quotations came from. Record your answers using this key:

S—Schwarzkopf Generation   **X**—Generation X
B—Baby Boomer   **Y**—Generation Y

Be prepared to shed some stereotypes. Answers are provided at the end of the test.

_____ 1. "I respect authority and follow the rules—but that authority has to earn my respect by being ethical and fair. Otherwise, I will do all I can do to circumvent the rules."

_____ 2. "I think working from home is a bad idea. Out of sight, out of mind."

_____ 3. "I wouldn't want [my managers] to be intimidating, but at the same time I want them to display that they have more knowledge than me. I want my bosses to respect me, but I also want to feel challenged by them. I don't want to feel like I'm on the same level as them. You want to look up to your bosses and feel that there is something you can learn from them. But at the same time, I want to be able to be comfortable around them."

_____ 4. "The quality of my work is very important to me, and I want to be appreciated for that. I have other priorities besides my work; namely, family and faith. I prefer to work in a team environment. I need to feel that I'm making a difference in someone's life. I have a strong sense of loyalty to what I do and who I do it for." ➡

Generational I.Q. Test *(concluded)*

_____ 5. "I'd rather be the authority than be subject to it."

_____ 6. "Above all else, I want my life to make a positive difference. I place a high value on learning—both academic and experiential. I am mistrustful of 'the System,' but expect government to play an active role in social services. Change is inevitable—it's both a challenge and a pleasure. Change is difficult but exciting."

_____ 7. "When it's all said and done at retirement, I want to look back and be able to say that I was happy with my choices."

_____ 8. "I still feel more comfortable with the hierarchy. But I want to be able to have input in decisions. I want my input to be considered."

_____ 9. "I want lots of free rein in a creative, flexible, non-traditional environment and [to] be treated with utmost trust, or else forget it—I'm leaving to find security and recognition elsewhere."

_____ 10. "Ideally, I wouldn't have a boss, but someone who assigns projects and gives me free rein—some kind of guidance, especially when I am new to the job, but free rein to do as I see fit and as I think is best. I will be responsible for the consequences, but let me do my own thing with as little supervision as possible."

Answers: 1. B; 2. S; 3. Y; 4. B; 5. X; 6. B; 7. X; 8. S; 9. B; 10. Y.

PART ONE
Who's in Your
Generation Mix Today?

What You Can Expect

WHAT SHAPES A GENERATION is infinitely complex. Many experts have written about that complexity in depth by detailing the historical events that define the generations and their members. Here we provide an executive summary: quick historical snapshots, one for each generation, focused on the beliefs, attitudes, and perspectives of each generation. We also take a look at each generation's early workplace experiences and then focus on where each generation is headed today.

Next, we offer you the most effective best practices we've discovered about leading and managing each cohort given their current needs and expectations. We also identify the urgent "strategic imperatives" that you and your organization must address if you want to attract, recruit, and retain the best talent of each generation.

Finally, we outline an interactive training exercise that will help your team members expand the awareness and understanding of their own generation as well as that of others. This discussion will be an important first step in creating a collaborative team. It will help your team break down age-related barriers of misunderstanding and misperception and will clear the path to more effective learning, greater productivity, and more lively innovation than ever before.

Chapter I

The Schwarzkopf Generation: Take Charge and Do What's Right

"I have allegiance to this country and its values as demonstrated in the workplace. I respect control leadership, my elders, and those who fought for my freedom. I believe we are responsible for our actions."

—A sixtysomething physical therapist

FOR OUR SENIOR GENERATION (those born before 1946), we have adopted the term "Schwarzkopf Generation" in honor of General Norman Schwarzkopf, commander of the allied forces in Operation Desert Shield/Storm. Shortly after that war, Bruce's path began to cross General Schwarzkopf's on the speaking circuit at various corporate conferences. The General would be there to present his generation's approach to leadership, while Bruce would speak about Generation X. Time and again, General Schwarzkopf would explain that for him, it all came down to two rules:

1. When in command, take charge.
2. When in doubt, do what's right.

"Take charge" and "Do what's right." Those imperatives define the expectations and attitudes of the oldest generation in the workplace today, those whom we respectfully call the Schwarzkopfers.

Historical Snapshot

Schwarzkopfers are "betweeners." Born too late to participate in the mettle-testing event of World War II and too early to become full-blown flower children, they found themselves stuck between "can do" Veterans and "I gotta be me" Boomers. Always one step out of sync with the times, Schwarzkopfers were young adults when it was hip to be teenagers. They were in their thirties when you couldn't trust anyone over thirty. They were in their forties when flower children proclaimed, "Make love, not war." Some experimented with free love—and found it wasn't so "free." (Divorce rates among their cohort began to soar in the 1970s.) Some discovered mind-expanding drugs (or, as a sixtysomething once chuckled, "better living through chemistry.") Most embraced the conformist *Ozzie and Harriet, Father Knows Best* homogenized world of the 1950s.

Schwarzkopfers were awed by the sacrifices that the "Greatest Generation" made to ensure a world "safe for democracy." They adopted their elders' values of loyalty, dedication, and commitment to command/control leadership within hierarchical organizations. With their outer-focused "we" attitude, they helped rebuild the American economy in the 50s and looked forward to the ultimate rewards: status as an all-American family owning its own home, lifetime employment in a solid organization, and a comfortable retirement. They even had their own war—Korea.

While Schwarzkopfers still hold some of the most important positions in business and politics today, they have never had a U.S. President emerge from their ranks. Walter Mondale, Michael Dukakis, and Jack Kemp were passed over for Veterans (Ronald Reagan and George H. W. Bush

---

And Let Us Not Forget

We must acknowledge a small but powerful group of social activists and artists within the Schwarzkopf Generation who have had a dramatic impact on U.S. history. The radical counterbalance to their conservative colleagues, they include the major leaders of the great social movements of the 60s such as Martin Luther King, Jr., Caesar Chavez, and Gloria Steinem, as well as the first Students for a Democratic Society members and the first Peace Corps volunteers.

Add to that list Elvis Presley, James Dean, Bob Dylan, Andy Warhol, and Ralph Nader, and you have an idea of the scope of their influence and contribution.

---

or Boomers (Bill Clinton and George W. Bush). Playing the role of supporting cast (Jim Baker, John Sununu, Madeline Albright, Dick Cheney, and Colin Powell), they have been brilliant advisors, mediators, and aides. They are known for their human relationship skills and their ability to negotiate, prompting some experts to call them the "helpmate" generation.

Schwarzkopfers Go to Work

Having started their working lives in the 1950s and 1960s, Schwarzkopfers built their careers during an era when the belief in job security made sense. Many followed the old-fashioned career path, making lots of short-term sacrifices in exchange for promised rewards that vested in the long term. They embodied the loyalty, commitment, and "an honest day's work for an honest day's pay" ethic they inherited from the Veterans. And they thought others should, too.

Although they initially emulated their elders' "command-and-control" leadership style, many Schwarzkopfer managers eventually softened the more rigid model of "When I say jump, you ask, 'How high?'" They were more likely to make room for participation in problem solving and decision making than their elders were, and many Schwarzkopfer workers wanted to participate.

As an office manager in the timber-products industry explains, "I still feel more comfortable with the hierarchy, but I want to be able to have input in decisions and I want my input to be considered."

Schwarzkopfers are also more patient with mediating conflicts through "processing" and gathering opinions than their "give me the bottom line fast" Gen X colleagues. This "process" versus "product" approach often causes conflict when, for example, they try to train Gen Xers and Yers.

A sixtysomething told us, "Today younger people expect us to spout 'pearls of wisdom,' but they're impatient when we try to train them. I have to realize that they've 'gotten it' long before I think they have. They don't want the 'story'; they want to know the bottom line: How do you do it? Yet, sometimes I have to give them the background 'why' so they have the guiding principles to work from when I'm not around."

"Guiding principles," standardized policies, procedures, templates. Years of experience have taught Schwarz-kopfers to rely on those tried and true ways of doing things, and many would still agree, "If it's not broken, don't fix it." In fact, they still thrive on standard operating procedures, both written and verbal.

Paradoxically, despite their reputation as change resisters, many members of this generation became true change masters of the workforce. If they seemed skeptical about a new idea, it might be because they were remembering when it was a "new idea" 30 years ago . . . and then again 20 years ago . . . and then again 10 years ago. Their institutional memory remains an invaluable compass to steer your organization, your team, and your career through today's minefield of constant change. While their "Been there, done that" attitude may initially rankle, remember this: To understand the new, you must study the old.

Schwarzkopfers at Work Today

In the early 2000s, many Schwarzkopfers were still wondering if Xers and Yers would ever adopt a strong work ethic. Some were having a hard time understanding job hoppers and had little patience with anyone unwilling to make sacrifices for an organization. Others were wary of those who rebelled against the dues-paying and ladder-climbing paradigm they had always known. And most were still hoping to cash out their investments in the old-fashioned workplace bargain and live out their golden years in a secure retirement.

Today, Schwarzkopfers find it vaguely insulting, but mostly inconvenient, that their young colleagues won't happily do all the grunt work, be last in line for every perk, and make no demands. On the other hand, they know that today's young workers would be fools to pay their dues and climb the ladder the old-fashioned way. This realization makes most Schwarzkopfers feel a little sad, but not as sad as they feel watching their hard-earned pensions and health-care benefits dwindle or disappear.

Schwarztkopfer Free Agency

A 68-year-old retired nurse told us that her local hospital wouldn't accept her application to work part-time on a 7 p.m. to 11 p.m. shift.

"They told me I wouldn't get anything done in four hours," she sighed. "I told them, with my experience, I could do more in four hours than most of their staff could do in eight! But they wouldn't hire me."

"So what are you doing now?" we asked.

"Well," she perked up. "I work for several doctors' offices educating their senior patients about the proper use of medications. And, I advise real estate agents about 'senior friendly' properties and how to make them attractive to older people. I charge an hourly rate."

"Then you're a free agent who owns your own business!"

"Well, I guess I am," she pondered, and then smiled. "I guess I am."

Some will be severely disappointed by—and outraged at—organizations to which they dedicated their lives. A t-shirt worn by a retired airlines employee proclaimed his generation's lifelong expectation: "Pensions are promises that cannot be broken." However, for many Schwarzkopfers, what they thought was money in the bank has been reduced to a broken promise.

Maybe that's what this generation means today when they say, "Loyalty is dead." The verbal potshot they first aimed at Generation X is now a harsh salvo fired at their own organizations.

Holding on to the last vestiges of the workplace of the past, Schwarzkopfers who have earned seniority tend to feel strongly that their longevity should be valued and rewarded. Still, by necessity, many of them are thinking like free agents too: "What's the deal around here for me today?" They too have to take care of their lives and their families. Organizations no longer will do that for them.

How to Manage Schwarzkopfers

Schwarzkopfers tell us two things stand out as most important in their working lives: the work itself and the people they work with. Unlike younger employees, they don't demand any "deep" meaning from their jobs—that was originally a Boomer imperative. For Schwarzkopfers, work must be satisfying in and of itself, make a contribution to the organization, and reflect their skills and expertise. With this in mind, you can capitalize on the strengths of our most experienced generation through five basic management practices:

1. Ask about the work itself—and offer learning experiences.
2. Make it clear: No "coasting" allowed.
3. Address the new standard of customization.
4. Encourage "making the call."
5. Create knowledge transfer programs.

1. Ask About the Work Itself— and Offer Learning Experiences

When was the last time you had a conversation about job satisfaction with your Schwarzkopf employees? With all the attention paid to younger workers, managers sometimes overlook the importance of touching base with their experienced people about the very reason they come to work every day: to do an important job very well. And if you're one of those managers who accepts as fact the entrenched stereotype that older workers don't want to learn new skills or have new experiences, it's time for a big change. The truth is, current research confirms just the opposite: Many Schwarzkopfers want to remain mentally agile and challenged and are ready for new experiences when offered the opportunity.

To get on course with this generation, your first step is to have a one-on-one conversation with each Schwarzkopfer on your team and ask questions such as the following:

- What work would you like to be doing more of? Less of?

- Are there any talents you aren't using right now that would benefit the team? The organization? How could you begin using them immediately?

- If you could redefine your job to make it more satisfying, what would it look like?

- What new skills would you want to learn to enhance your job performance?

- Are there any leadership opportunities you'd be interested in pursuing? If so, what would it take to get you up to speed to tackle them?

- How can I recognize and reward you for the contributions you make to the team?

Always remember: Learning never ends, and can be an especially good investment with loyal Schwarzkopfers. Unlike Xers or Yers, who want to amass skills they can leverage *elsewhere* someday, this cohort wants to learn new skills to be more effective and valued in their *present* jobs. They wish to keep contributing to the companies for which many of them have worked 25-plus years. Considering such loyalty, it's disturbing that a survey of 150 HR executives revealed 75 percent of them didn't use ongoing training as a motivator for older workers. That's a mistake you can't afford to make.

Studies have shown that the human mind doesn't slow down until after age 70. Therefore, trainers who are willing to teach "new tricks" to Schwarzkopfers in a "safe" environment—one in which older workers don't feel embarrassed or put on the spot—and know how to match the pace and learning styles of these workers have great success.

This means encouraging everyone, even some Schwarzkopfers themselves, to discard the stereotype that "you can't teach an old dog new tricks." Typically what feeds this stereotype today are the challenges that new technologies can pose to older workers. Granted, most of these workers have not been as mentally hardwired as younger people to pick up tech-related skills in a snap; but as successes in libraries and senior centers around the country attest, even the oldest members of this cohort can master the basics with patience and practice.

2. Make It Clear: No "Coasting" Allowed

Recent research also shows that older workers are often more engaged with their work, and therefore more motivated to exceed expectations, than are younger workers. Yet at times we hear managers complain that certain Schwarzkopfers are sitting back, producing little, and biding their time until retirement. Don't allow these workers—or anyone on your team, for that matter—to "coast." Hold every Schwarzkopfer accountable for ambitious goals just as you would any other employee.

If coasting is a problem, try to discover why the problem has developed. People coast for any number of reasons. For example, previous managers may have tolerated this behavior, letting it become a workplace norm; or perhaps these workers see little or no opportunity to learn new things and so are bored. You need to be the manager who challenges the coasting culture by finding out what's behind the lethargy; then you can re-ignite the fire in your Schwarzkopfers by "taking charge," offering them ambitious goals and new opportunities, and holding them accountable every step of the way.

Always back up this approach by rigorously offering individual feedback for improvement, and by basing rewards solely on performance. Meet with these workers regularly to problem-solve, troubleshoot, and provide resources and coaching. Let "coasters" know in no uncertain terms that pre-retirement exit strategies are available if they continue to choose this course of inaction.

At the Top of Their Game . . .

With Americans living longer and healthier lives, Schwarz-kopfers are dramatically redefining who a "senior" is and what he or she can do. For example:

- Forty-six athletes, including two women in their nineties, competed in the United States Tennis Association's National Women's 70-80-90 Indoor Championships in August 2005.

- CVS, the drugstore chain, reports they currently have people in their seventies lifting heavy boxes and those in their nineties engaged in challenging management positions.

- The cover of *Business Week,* June 27, 2005, spotlighted two sixtysomethings and a 92-year-old. The headline proclaimed: "Old. Smart. Productive."

Understand that if you're the first manager who has taken such a proactive approach, these workers may initially resent your attempts to re-engage them. However, muster the guts and courage to keep at it. One of the most damaging messages you can send to your team is that it's okay to retire from doing significant work months—or even years—before they retire from the organization. And one of the most demotivating messages you can send your older workers is that mediocre or poor performance is acceptable.

3. Address the New Standard of Customization

Another management imperative is to convince this generation that the new standard in the twenty-first-century workplace is customization. The one-size-fits-all paradigm of solutions and strategies that worked so well in the past is gone. Customization of everything—from products and services to working arrangements—is in, and that requires more fluid, flexible policies and procedures as well as the willingness of everyone on the team to use his or her best judgment, day to day, moment to moment.

Remember, this generation depends on standard operating procedures and clear policies and guidelines. With that in mind, engage your Schwarzkopfers in a process of reviewing the procedures, policies, and guidelines that make an impact on their work. Ask them to determine which remain valid today and which need updating. Consider the following four-step process:

Step 1. Ask your Schwarzkopfers to make a list of all the tasks and responsibilities they are charged with accomplishing and have direct experience with.

Step 2. Have them prioritize their tasks and responsibilities according to importance and frequency.

Step 3. Ask them to create standard operating procedures (SOPs) for each task and responsibility, beginning with their top priority. Tell them you are looking for clear, concise, step-by-step explanations for what they do and how they achieve the best results.

Step 4. Review each SOP to ensure that processes are up-to-date, given new technology and the latest policies and procedures.

Obviously, this process may take weeks or months to accomplish, but don't let that deter you or them. Make the case to Schwarzkopfers that they are significantly contributing to the department by updating and document-ing work models both for training new hires and for ongoing learning opportunities for their teammates. And, of course, find ways to recognize and reward them for their contributions.

4. Encourage "Making the Call"

Schwarzkopfers who have amassed years of experience have a broader context in which to make business decisions, but they need your support, encouragement, and recognition to do so. After decades of working under command-and-control management, it will take time to convince them you are serious when you say, "Make the call," "Use your own judgment," and "I'll stand behind you, no matter what the outcome." Building this kind of supportive, trusting environment is imperative because one of the most important workplace relationships this generation has is with you, their manager.

Taking a cue from their Veteran heroes, Schwarzkopfers want to work with strong leaders who have proven track records. They have the expectation that leaders "take charge" and "do what's right." They don't mind having "a boss" as long as that person respects their input and involves them in decision making.

If you're a young manager, you're initially in a precarious position. You need to convince Schwarzkopfers that you have enough industry knowledge, self-confidence, and people skills to deserve your leadership role. You also need to assure them that you need their wisdom and experience to shorten your learning curve and make you a better manager. A savvy Gen X manager quickly gained the support of a respected Schwarzkopf staffer when she told him, "I bet you never dreamed you'd be working for someone young enough to be your daughter. But I've been appointed to this position, and I'm going to do everything I can to help us all succeed. I'll need your experience and wisdom to help me do that. Can I count on you?"

Schwarzkopfers, with their strong work ethic, can be counted on. If you respectfully assert your authority and genuinely utilize their expertise, you will have success. Remember that they are great helpers and supporters and will be an integral part of your generation mix until the moment they retire—and beyond.

Note: Since more younger managers than ever before are responsible for older direct reports, we address this trend in more depth in Chapter 11.

5. Create Knowledge Transfer Programs

As one million Schwarzkopfers exit the workplace every year, the greatest legacy they can leave an organization is their experience, knowledge, and wisdom. They are bonafide knowledge workers, and you can't afford to have them walk out the door with what they've learned during their tenure with your organization.

During one of our Generation Mix workshops, we learned that at least a hundred managers and employees in a state agency would be retiring within the next year. The HR director in the room confirmed that fact, so we asked, "Have you started knowledge transfer yet?" The response? Silence followed by a sheepish question: "Oh, should we?"

In contrast, we were discussing the issue of knowledge transfer with a federal government association. Afterwards, a fiftysomething manager told us, "I just realized our director is retiring in three years. When I get back to work, I'm getting him started on transferring his knowledge immediately. He knows too much and we can't afford to let him go without learning what he knows."

One year? Three years? How much time do you have before Schwarzkopfer managers and employees leave your organization? The opportunity to capture what they know is now. How do you do that? By creating formal and informal knowledge transfer programs.

If you've engaged Schwarzkopfers in documenting the standard operating procedures we discussed above, you've already begun. Take the process a valuable step further by considering these tactics:

- Create a "go-to" list of Schwarzkopfer experts whom younger workers can contact when they need immediate information on a customer, client, process, project, or procedure. This list will also give Schwarzkopfers recognition for their experience and knowledge.

- Establish teams of Schwarzkopfers who do similar work, and engage them in generating answers to the most frequently asked questions they receive about the organization's products, services, or policies. Make these FAQs part of the training materials given to new hires.

- Bring together Schwarzkopfers who have experience handling difficult customers, and engage them in role-plays—or, at least, in creating real-life scripts others can dramatize—and videotape the results. These video clips become vignettes in your training library for teaching younger employers what to say and how to say it. One of the most valuable lessons older workers can share with younger workers is how to deal with all types of people respectfully and professionally.

- Engage Schwarzkopfers in coaching new hires on how to get up to speed more quickly. A nurse manager told us that senior nurses in her hospital work on the floor three days a week and spend the other two coaching new nurses on bedside skills. These are skills acquired through years of experience, not textbook or classroom learning.

  Other areas for coaching may include intangibles such as how to best navigate through red tape by finding the best allies in HR; how to determine which processes and procedures are non-negotiable and which are open to work-arounds; and how to communicate more effectively with certain clients or coworkers.

- Formalize job shadowing, cross training, and job-sharing opportunities so younger workers can experience the work Schwarzkopfers do up-close and personal.

- Engage interested Schwarzkopfers in becoming trainers of the skill sets they have mastered. Before they address a group, however, make sure they have the teaching skills they need to be successful. Find a master teacher who can offer "train the trainer" programs to get them up to speed.

Whatever routes you take to ensure knowledge transfer, set a precedent for recognizing, honoring, and rewarding

Schwarzkopfers for sharing their experience and wisdom. Be sure to ask these people themselves how they would like be rewarded for their contributions. Then, make knowledge transfer part of how you do business with members of all generations as you go through the Generational Shift.

Initiating Strategic Imperatives for the Schwarzkopf Generation

At your next managers' meeting, discuss the strategic imperatives for this generation. Which ones are so urgent that you need to tackle them immediately? What tactics do you need to implement so you are on the bleeding edge of these important Schwarzkopfer issues? Be sure to address the following:

- What negative stereotypes does our organization hold about Schwarzkopfers? How are we going to dispel those stereotypes by supporting the "truths" about this generation? How are we going to make this an age-friendly workplace for this generation?

- How much does our organization value and rely upon the experience of our older workers? When things go wrong, to whom do we turn to get things back on track? How do we publicly acknowledge and reward our Schwarzkopfers for their expertise?

- We need to begin the process of capturing and transferring the knowledge, skill, and wisdom of older workers immediately. How will we do that? How will we recognize and reward them for their contributions to the process?

- We need to redefine retirement and create flexible work programs so older workers will want to keep working for us. What would those programs look like? Which can we offer right now to Schwarzkopfers who are nearing retirement?

Note: Since the issue of retirement spans the Schwarzkopfer and Boomer generations—and will make an impact on younger generations for decades to come—we take a more in-depth look at this topic in Chapter 9.

Chapter 2

Baby Boomers:
Trendsetters to the End

Before long, the baby-boom generation—some of the '60s crowd is now in its 60s—will begin packing [nursing home] facilities. When old rock and rollers show up with their walkers—trendsetters to the end— the nursing homes might well become the hottest singles scene going.

> — Dirk Johnson and Julie Scelfo,
> "Sex, Love, and Nursing Homes,"
> *Newsweek,* December 15, 2003

MOST RESEARCHERS DEFINE the huge Baby Boom generation as those born between 1946 and 1964. However, every day we meet people born after 1953 who tell us they can't identify with the "old rock and rollers" and feel like proverbial fish out of water. Their voices have become too loud for us to ignore. While all Boomers share much in common—namely, a child-centered upbringing, a focus on individuality and youth, and a distrust of anyone in authority—there are enough differences between the first and second waves to make them distinct cohorts.

We thus divide the 61.5 million Boomers in the workforce into two groups. We call the first wave born between 1946 and 1953 the Woodstockers. Even if they didn't attend that event or participate in the hippie counterculture, they shared the idealism and optimism of the late 60s and early 70s. And, until history definitively names them, we'll simply identify those born between 1954 and 1964 as Young Boomers.

Historical Snapshot: The Woodstockers

Many chroniclers describe the Woodstock Generation as the original "Me Generation." Raised by doting, outer-focused World War II Veteran parents, they became "The New Breed": a spoiled, self-indulgent, entitled "Now" generation demanding immediate gratification. In contrast to previous generations, they enjoyed a particularly child-focused upbringing and, in retrospect, they claim to have invented "youth culture."

Unlike the Schwarzkopf Generation, Woodstockers were always in the right historical place at the right time. They were kids when it was cool to be a kid, teens when it was cool to be a teen. They were in their twenties when you couldn't trust anyone over thirty. By the time the oldest reached college in the mid 1960s, they were ready to rebel against the safe, secure, "ticky-tacky," rule-bound world their traditional parents had created. Not content to live in black-and-white "Pleasantville," where the parental imperative was "Get a good job and settle down," many set out not merely to define their individuality, but also to create a more open, free society. As a fiftysomething fire chief put it, "We did not rebel just because we could. We wanted something better—more real."

By the time they emerged from three major assassinations (those of Veteran John Fitzgerald Kennedy and Schwarzkopfers Robert Kennedy and Martin Luther King, Jr.), the Summer of Love, Kent State, and Vietnam, these older Boomers were becoming the "over-thirties" they said they'd never trust. They cut their hair, donned business suits, and slipped into the very Establishment they had railed against the decade before. With their dreams of a social revolution shattered, many Woodstockers channeled their energies into their work and a dual search for material goods and spirituality as a way to affirm their self-worth. For many, work became their identity, competition their driving force, and self-improvement a way of life.

Historical Snapshot: Young Boomers

Younger members of the Boomer cohort are now trying to establish themselves as another "betweener" generation. Too young to participate in more than the "feel" of Woodstock and the social rebellion of the 60s, they were nurtured on the high expectations of their hardworking Schwarzkopfer parents and their older Boomer siblings. What they reaped instead were the high disappointments of the 70s: Watergate, gas lines, the Iranian hostage crisis, a faltering economy. They learned early on that, of course, you can't trust politicians; that, of course, ideals don't easily translate into action; that, of course, you have to struggle to realize your dreams; that, of course, burning bras or violently protesting war doesn't get you what you want. In essence, harsh realities tempered any idealism their elders offered. But it also taught them that real change unfolds from the inside, not the outside.

As a fortysomething educator explained, "Martin Luther King, Jr. became our hero and taught us that we could make things better not by becoming 'boat shakers,' but by building a better boat. Many of us learned to make our voices heard through voting, through being 'politely political.' We have a sense of fairness, justice, and loyalty, but we're willing to be political if pushed."

Unlike the other generations surrounding them, however, Young Boomers never had a war of their own. They were too young for Vietnam and too old for Desert Storm.

Reflecting on their generation, a group of fortysomething HR professionals concluded: "We think we should call our generation the Bridgers or the Seekers. We are the bridge between older and younger generations, and we are seeking ambitious goals and dreams as we strive for work/life balance."

Boomers Go to Work

After their youthful rebellion, many Woodstockers grew up and settled down in the early to mid 1970s. Although Young Boomers were just graduating from high school or college at that time, both cohorts ultimately followed the same workplace path: They hitched their wagons to the star of an established organization and started paying their dues. Their bosses were real grown-ups who, like their parents, had standard operating procedures for everything. Command-and-control leadership was the norm, and while Boomers secretly mistrusted anyone in authority, they kept their heads down and worked hard. Most of the time, work was 'sink or swim,' so they had to figure out what to do and then do it. They didn't make demands. They waited for their bosses to notice their hard work and reward them in due course. They believed in job security and figured the system would take care of them through retirement.

But then, just as they started to earn seniority and move into positions of authority, they were hit by the downsizing daze of the late 80s and early 90s. Shell-shocked Boomers watched organizational hierarchies flatten, hundreds of thousands of jobs disappear, and the lifetime employment bubble burst. While some were strongly entrenched in secure positions, others were forced into the job-hopping mode Xers would see as "business as usual." A record number of them flatly rejected corporate America once and for all and set out to create their own businesses. Others stayed on board, struggling to do more with less, and championed teamwork and consensus as the way to meet their goals. Still others were cut adrift and spent months, even years, trying to reestablish themselves in their careers.

Whatever their situation, Boomers, whose personal identity was often defined by their work ("I am what I do" was a Boomer anthem), took a punch in the stomach of self-worth and self-esteem. Like Schwarzkopfers, they gradually realized that the loyalty they had given to their organizations was not reciprocal. Like Gen Xers, they finally "got it." A new HR director in a large Midwestern bank explained, "I understood what Gen X was all about when the company I worked with for 17 years let me go. I love my job right now, but I'm not sure I'll be retiring from it. I'm keeping my options open." By necessity, the most savvy Boomers became free agents.

As Boomers Go, So Goes the Workplace

Because there are so darned many Baby Boomers, today there is not a trend in the western world worth its salt that does not have a substantial following among Baby Boomers. If Boomers had rejected the "free agent" norms and values associated with Generation X and Generation Y, that trend would have dried up and blown away. But that's not what happened. It was when Baby Boomers of all ages embraced this new mindset that free agency became the unstoppable trend it is today.

The same will hold true during the next decade as Boomers redefine aging and retirement. For the first time in history, we have a generation who exhibits a powerful combination of forces: vigorous minds and bodies, vast life experience, mature perspectives, a life-expectancy of 83 years (according to health researchers, many will live well into their nineties), and a burning desire to answer the questions "Is that all there is? What's next? What do I want to 'be' as well as 'do' when I grow up?" Organizations who help Boomers answer those questions within the context of work will have a strategic advantage over those who cut ties with Boomers after they retire.

Boomers at Work Today

At 41.5 percent of the workforce, the Baby Boomer cohort still dominates the workplace today, with Woodstockers holding the lion's share of leadership positions in most organizations in most industries. Sounding very much like Schwarzkopfers, one group of older Boomers in the federal government proudly proclaimed, "We run the place! We remember history and context and are committed to the mission." Indeed, they have arrived.

In the early 2000s, we found that some Boomers were understandably conflicted over the many changes in the workplace. The rules were changing, nervy Xers were making demands these seasoned pros would never have dreamed of making, and those pesky Gen Yers were just arriving, expecting big league jobs with little league experience.

In reaction, some Woodstockers dug in their heels, resisting the changes and defining work as something they had to do in order to survive. Speaking for these "survivalists," a fiftysomething high school teacher described himself and his Woodstocker colleagues as the "dinosaurs" in their department: "We just trudge along following and enforcing the rules and regulations. Our out-of-school lives are quite limited. We put in the extra hours and give stability to the department. We're the first to arrive and the last to leave. We're cynical, yet we're the most loyal to the school."

Priding themselves on their ability to survive "sink or swim" management, the loyal, cynical "dinosaurs" of this cohort complained to us about bosses who spent too much time with young hires, and expressed anger over the incentives and training opportunities offered to new staffers.

In contrast, many Young Boomers sounded just like Xers and Yers. They told us they loved work as long as it was fun, provided opportunities for creativity, and allowed them to have a rich life outside of work. This group was gracefully making the transition into the new global workplace, embracing the flexibility, techno-literacy, and entrepreneurial thinking it demands. As the manager of a private law office put it, "I never anticipated the enormous impact of computers and technology, and how together they would allow me to succeed in a demanding job while at the same time (nearly!) succeeding in having a fulfilling personal life. I work from home roughly 20 percent of the time, and rarely miss a beat in the ebb and flow of office life."

Young Boomers were also redefining one of the favorite buzzwords of the 90s: *empowerment.* Rather than looking to a long-term career path in an organization as a source of power, or to some vague feel-good sense of 'personal' power, they realized that they needed to find ways to make themselves powerful in order to take care of themselves and their families. They started taking responsibility for their own careers, realizing that they were free agents whether they wanted to be or not.

Working for Balance

Fewer and fewer Boomers of all ages today are willing to keep up the frenetic pace that made them ideal foot soldiers in the 70s and 80s. Young Boomers, in particular, have been lobbying for family-friendly workplaces and work/life balance initiatives for a decade. When the Woodstocker CEO of a multinational corporation proclaimed that, given the stressful demands of their fiercely competitive market-place, managers should accept the fact that "balance" was out of the question for this organization, a fortysomething shot back, "You better think about that again because we will lose productivity—not gain it—if we're not taking care of our people."

Boomers Discard Corporate "Boxes"

Carl Camden, COO of Kelly Services, estimates that 42 percent of American workers of all ages were looking for a new job in 2005. Why? Many wanted a better balance between work and lifestyle. With consultants, temps, independent contractors, and freelancers now making up 22 percent of the workforce and becoming its fastest-growing segment, he predicts that Baby Boomers will become the majority of free agent employees in the future.

In addition, according to Deborah R. Russell, Director for Economic Security for AARP (the 36-million-member voice of the 50-plus set), 40 percent of the self-employed population in 2002 were over the age of 50. Given Boomers' entrepreneurial impulses, that number will spike in the future as they reach retirement age.

In reaction to the work addiction of their older siblings, Young Boomers emphasize family values and a balanced life among their strengths. Leaving work at work and tending to interests outside their careers have become essential to their lifestyle—and they're proud of it. A forty-something job services representative put it this way: "The quality of my work is very important to me, and I want to be appreciated for that, but I have other priorities besides work, namely, my family and faith."

Endless research confirms that "face time" at work alone does not immediately correlate with productivity. In fact, people who reduce work hours to spend more time with their families are often more productive because they bring more energy, commitment, and attention to their jobs. Getting eight hours of sleep each night, knowing you

---

In the Spotlight—Again!

The most chronicled generation in history did it again.
The cover of *Newsweek,* November 14, 2005, announced:
"Ready or Not, Boomers Turn 60." It pictured celebrities
such as Tommy Lee Jones, Ben Vereen, Connie Chung,
Jann Wenner, Oliver Stone, Donald Trump, Susan Sarandon,
Diane Keaton, Dolly Parton, Sylvester Stallone, Bill Clinton,
Diane Sawyer, George W. and Laura Bush, Liza Minnelli,
and Linda Rondstadt.

Newsweek also announced that "Boomer Files" would
become a regular feature during 2006.

---

can work from home when your child or elderly parent is
ill, and having the leeway to deal with personal issues all
lend themselves to better results in less stressed-out work
environments.

Since downsizing is still a daily reality and some organizations are still "trading in" high-salaried Boomers for less
expensive younger workers, the emphasis on free agency,
self-loyalty, and self-responsibility will continue to be a
Boomer imperative. "I take calls from headhunters all the
time," admits a fortysomething advertising director for a
multimillion-dollar corporation. "I know I'm only a 'hired gun.'
If my major account folds, I'm out of work, so it's important
for me to know what's out there."

Now entering their sixties, Woodstocker trendsetters are
already redefining retirement and, typically, doing it their
way. Alongside Schwarzkopfers, they've set out to expand
upon and entrench the emerging trends in retirement that
will have an impact on generations to come. Many

Boomers—including those in their forties—tell us they are preparing to retire. But most also tell us they will NEVER stop working. They're already reinventing retirement as a hodgepodge of part-timing, flex-timing, temp working, job sharing, telecommuting, freelancing, consulting, and entrepreneuring.

Note: A closer examination of this topic is presented in Chapter 9.

How to Manage Boomers

Ask Boomers of all ages what's important to them at work, and you'll hear three things: respect, respect, respect.

- Respect for their contributions
- Respect for their skills, knowledge, and wisdom
- Respect for what they can still offer organizations before they "retire"

Like Schwarzkopfers, Boomers have been around for decades. Many have earned high levels of credibility within their organizations. They paid their dues in the old workplace and want to be recognized for their contributions in the new.

However, some managers, in their attempts to engage Xers and Yers, have overlooked the expertise of their Boomer employees. A fiftysomething elementary school teacher put it bluntly: "Our principal is falling all over Gen Yers, who I agree are sharp. But in the process, she's discounting Boomer teachers who have made this school great and who could serve as mentors to these young

A Case Study in Boomer Free Agency

Everyday we meet Boomers who proudly tell us that Gen Xers and Yers have nothing on them. Some were job hoppers in their youth, others were free agents without ever having heard the term, and most recognized from the start of their working lives that career success rested in their own hands.

One outstanding role model is our friend and colleague—we'll call him Mr. Blue—who is in an educational leadership role with a large federal agency. This upbeat, talented Boomer created a dream job within a large bureaucracy—a job that offers him a flexible schedule, creative opportunities to build experiential learning classes, and a cadre of enthusiastic colleagues to support his efforts. ("Take any of these away and I'd have to seriously rethink my retirement date," Blue quips.)

A free agent from day one, Blue recognized that his success within the agency would depend on creating his own opportunities for career advancement and establishing a high level of credibility. So he diversified his skills with graduate degrees and set about to effect major changes within the agency culture.

Nine years ago, after 19 years of stacking up successes, Blue moved into his current role. As an education leader, he created a management development program for the agency's Northeast region that is the envy of the entire organization.

Now facing retirement, Blue is ensuring his success is passed on to others. He's already training facilitators to carry on his innovative programs and being very selective about who will take his place. At the same time, he's picking his own work assignments carefully so that he can spend more time with his family and perfect his fishing skills.

Like many Boomers, Mr. Blue has "gotten it" about work/life balance and the real meaning of empowerment. In addition, he's leaving behind a lasting legacy that will make an impact on generations within the agency for years to come.

people. What she doesn't know is, Yers are going to leave for other opportunities because her leadership is so poor. They are all 'flash and dash.' We will still be here. And we are not happy."

No wonder some Boomers are not happy. They're used to being in the spotlight, and they resent being discounted after decades of service. As a Gen Mix manager, then, your challenge is to balance your enthusiasm for new workers with genuine respect for the contributions of your Boomer staffers. How do you demonstrate that respect? Not surprisingly, this generation has definite ideas about that. Here's what they expect from their managers:

1. Honor their historical memory.
2. Give them recognition.
3. Let them try out new ideas.
4. Help bridge the team-individual divide.
5. Coach and challenge.

1. Honor Their Historical Memory

Like Schwarzkopfers, Boomers can put a contextual spin on why certain policies or procedures are non-negotiable for safety or legal reasons, or why certain approaches or innovations just won't work. We've heard them remind younger generations that faster is not always better. Taking the time to think things through rather than being the first one out of the gate often provides a strategic advantage. We've heard them recount the struggles they've faced trying to make significant policy changes or get approval for new technologies. We've watched them temper the feisty impatience of Gen Yers who demanded immediate "work-arounds" that wouldn't have worked at all.

Encourage your Boomers to make the distinction between "We're doing this because we've always done it this way" and "We're doing this because it's a safety issue"—or legal issue or change they've long been fighting for. Then, make sure they convey that history to their younger colleagues.

2. Give Them Recognition

This means honoring their opinions, skills, knowledge, potential, and contributions. Recognition has always been a Boomer imperative, yet few old-style leaders, who thought a salary was recognition enough, provided it. Even the most basic signs of appreciation and encouragement were rare. A veteran teacher told us she was pleasantly surprised when a new principal thanked her for being such a valuable professional on his staff. "No one, in all my 27 years of teaching, ever thanked me for my contributions." Don't let that happen to your valuable Boomers. From "Atta-boys" to spot bonuses, from a high-visibility assignment to a paid day off for extraordinary performance, find appropriate ways to honor these long-term contributors.

Finally, remember that a basic way to honor your Boomers is to listen to them, individually and as a team, and genuinely factor their ideas into your decision-making process. Some Boomers tell us they feel overlooked by managers who take them for granted and spend time and energy engaging Xers and Yers. Don't be counted among those managers.

3. Let Them Try Out New Ideas

Offer Boomers the flexibility and authority to experiment, and support them if they fail. Tap into the Boomer entrepreneurial impulse. Having been in the trenches for years, they have perspectives that can lead to important innovations.

4. Help Bridge the Team-Individual Divide

Understand that many Boomers are driven by conflicting impulses: the urge to compete to get ahead of the pack, and the desire to lead or participate on a productive team. You must help them decide which is the greater priority: distinguishing themselves or doing what's best for the team. Your best strategy may be to convince them that focusing on the team in the short term is the most effective way to distinguish themselves in the long term.

5. Coach and Challenge

Become a coach who facilitates goals, not dictates them, and who challenges Boomers to grow. Remember, self-improvement is a major aspiration of this cohort.

Offer coaching-style feedback on a consistent basis so your Boomers know what they're doing well and what they need to fix or improve upon, and provide guidelines for improvement with specific goals and deadlines.

Be sure to discuss new projects Boomers would like to explore, new skills they want to learn, and leadership opportunities they'd like to pursue. While it's true that the majority of new leaders will come from Generations X and Y, recognize that there are some Boomers ready, willing, and very capable of taking on leadership positions, perhaps for the first time in their careers. Keep challenging them—and then challenge them some more.

Also, make sure you're challenging your Boomers to mentor high-potential Xers and Yers. Let Boomers know you value their experience and need them to share their skills and knowledge. Boomers pride themselves on being "change leaders," and one of the most urgent changes today is moving everyone of all ages away from the "this is my power, my knowledge, my skills" paradigm to the cross-generational partnerships needed for successful collaboration.

As with the members of any other generation, Boomers want to be seen and treated as individuals. They value creating personal relationships and building rapport. Spend time getting to know them individually and divest yourself of the assumptions you have about people in their forties, fifties, and early sixties. (Even if you fall into one of those age groups, you still may hold stereotypes about them.) Examine your perceptions about what they can and cannot do and about the dreams and aspirations they "should" have at this stage in their lives. This dynamic cadre of professionals may surprise you.

Since Boomers will play significant roles on your Gen Mix team for the next five to 15 years, you can't afford to have them remain "not happy." Most have admirable track records and a strong work ethic; many are ready to become mentors to their younger colleagues. Unless they feel respected and recognized for their accomplishments, however, you will have little success getting them to work collaboratively.

Worksheet: Managing Boomers

Directions: List the name of each Boomer you manage. Then, in the appropriate columns, answer these questions: How effectively do you show each respect in the ways mentioned above? How could you become more effective in the future? How effective are you as a coaching-style manager? How could you become a better coach with each Boomer you manage?

Boomers	My "Respect" Ability	My Coaching Ability

Initiating Strategic Imperatives for Baby Boomers

At your next managers' meeting, discuss the strategic imperatives for this cohort. Which ones are so urgent that you need to tackle them immediately? What tactics do you need to implement so you are on the bleeding edge of these important Boomer issues? Be sure to address the following:

- How can we make our workplace age-friendly for people in their forties, fifties, and sixties?

- How much does our organization value and rely upon the experience of our Boomer workers? How do we publicly acknowledge and reward our Boomers for their expertise?

- We need to identify talented Boomer workers who are nearing retirement. How can we help them redefine retirement so their skills and talents stay with us for as long as possible? How do we include them in succession planning and knowledge transfer?

- Which older Boomers in our organization hold leadership positions? How do we encourage them to identify and develop high-potential employees so there will be enough bench strength to take over leadership roles as they retire? How we will recognize and reward these current leaders for their development skills?

Boomers have the potential to impact the workplace for decades to come, whether as full-timers, part-timers, mentors, coaches, freelancers, consultants, volunteers— or in any number of work relationships still to be created. They didn't come into the world quietly after World War II, and they have no intention of disappearing quietly into the twilight. This generational powerhouse is already precipitating a revolution that is forcing every organization to rethink the definitions of aging and retirement. And, given the fact that Boomers will indeed remain trendsetters to the end, there's no better generation to lead the charge.

Chapter 3

Generation X:
What's the Deal Today?

*"We are products of high divorce rates, the 80s
Reaganomics era, and post-war parents. Every day
we are making efforts [to create] well-being and a
safe future by working on environmental issues,
social acceptance, and lower crime rates."*

—A Gen X biotechnician in forestry

Historical Snapshot

A GENERATION OF LATCHKEY KIDS, Xers were born during
one of the most blatantly anti-child phases in U.S. history.
Their Schwarzkopfer and Woodstocker parents had the
highest divorce and abortion rates, highest number of dual-
income families, and most permissive parenting habits in
our history. Viewed as intrusive obstacles to their parents'
self-exploration, Xers found themselves in a faltering
economy that plunged them into the highest child-poverty
rates—and, later in their lives, the lowest wage and
homeownership rates—since the Great Depression. In fact,
they were the first generation of Americans to be told that
they would not be as well off financially as their parents.

Having grown up in the aftermath of their parents' social
rebellion, many Xers never developed strong connections

to the traditional institutions (churches, schools, corpora-tions, political parties) that had anchored their parents' coming of age. As a result, they became wary of institutions and learned early on that the only real security in a scary world lay within their own resourcefulness. And, indeed, during their formative years, the world was a terrifying place, even without a major war. Milk-carton kids became their MIAs. The AIDS epidemic put the lid on sexuality. Headlines screamed not of terrors abroad, but of those lurking down the street: Son of Sam, sexual abuse at home and in daycare centers, police brutality.

The most unsupervised generation, Xers were left to take care of themselves and developed a fierce "I've got to fend for myself" attitude. They grew into independent, goal-oriented, entrepreneurial thinkers whose ease with information and technology became one of their most important survival skills.

Generation X Goes to Work

In the late 80s, when Gen Xers first arrived in the work-place, things were already radically changing. With globalization and technology driving businesses into erratic markets and staffing practices, they quickly learned that job security was a relic from the past. When "lean and mean" employers told Schwarzkopfers and Boomers who had dedicated their lives to these enterprises, "Go take care of yourselves; we're not responsible for you," Xers took that message to heart. They understood from day one of their working lives that large institutions couldn't be trusted to make good on long-term promises. So, for short-term sacrifices, they demanded immediate gratification. They turned away from the traditional career path and its norms of success, acting like free agents. They began asking, "What's the deal around here today? What do you want from me today? What do I get in return today?"

At first, this free agency attitude was seen as a youthful aberration. Older managers assured one another, "They'll get over it soon and grow up." But then, the tech boom took off and turned into the dot.com craze. All of a sudden, Xers were viewed as super-workers who could leap tall buildings in a single keystroke and create magical business models that did not need products, services, or customers.

By the late 1990s, when unemployment stood at record lows and the war for talent raged on, this cohort became the most sought-after workforce. Independent, techno-savvy, entrepreneurial, adaptable, results-oriented: Xers had all the characteristics that made them attractive to organizations fast-forwarding into a global, technological, fiercely competitive marketplace.

But the tables turned again. By April 2000, good business news turned into bad business news; September 11, 2001, exacerbated the downward economic spiral; and it was déjà vu all over again for Xers. At this moment in history, many older business leaders and managers still expected the free agency trend to disappear, especially since those pesky Gen Xers were growing up and needed work. "They have more adult responsibilities now—surely Xers are finally seeking more security," these sage leaders reassured one another.

And, of course, Gen Xers were seeking security, but that security was still found where Xers always knew it must reside: in themselves, in their own self-building career security. In fact, the free agency mindset didn't disappear in the bad news years; it went mainstream. As we pointed out earlier, as the 2000s began to unfold, members of all generations learned they had to be true free agents in the great tradition of self-reliance, not because they wanted to, but because they had to. They had to take care of themselves and their families. Organizations weren't going to do it for them.

Generation X at Work Today

Now Gen Xers are no longer the new kids on the block. More than 22 percent of the workforce is younger than the youngest Xer. Meanwhile, the oldest Xers reached a milestone in 2005: They turned 40. Xers may be frustrated by the newest upstarts, Generation Y, but they are now the "adults" who become wistful when thinking about their own youthful rebellion.

Coming of age during the mythic new economy, Xers are the first generation to reach mature adulthood in the real new economy of highly interconnected, rapidly changing, fiercely competitive, knowledge-driven global markets. They are having the peculiar experience of watching their youthful responses prove wise and become mainstream. It was not their idealistic belief in magical business models and foosball tables in the teaming space that proved precocious; rather, it was their cynical mistrust of institutions and resolve to fend for themselves that was so prescient.

Xers today are still understandably cautious as they navigate the unpredictable world of work. They expect little from established institutions, but now they know how to squeeze out learning opportunities, relationship opportunities, creative challenges, financial rewards, and work/life balance by selling their time, energy, and creativity. In essence, they remain the consummate free agents who continue to test organizational waters: "Are my talents being used? Am I learning new skills I can leverage wherever I go? Am I being recognized and rewarded for my contributions today, not five years from now? Do I receive the feedback today that I need to stay on track and improve?"

Xers also know their security rests in staying on the bleeding edge. "Jobs may come and jobs may go, but my career belongs to me" remains the Xer anthem—one, by the way, that many Boomers have echoed since the early 2000s. Xers recognize that they were not the real children of the information revolution—they grew up as television went from seven channels to 57—but they also realize nowadays that what you know is less important than how quickly you learn new things and put them into action. Xers still don't care for "the way we do things around here," and continue to push their innovative spirit and entrepreneurial ideas. In fact, they remain great entrepreneurs and will start businesses like wildfire in the next decade.

Not surprisingly, Gen Xers heartily denounce their "slacker" stereotype. "We are not lazy!" proclaimed a thirtysomething employment director. They perceive themselves as hard-working, open-minded, and independent. They want to be productive at work, working smarter not harder, and to have fun in the process.

However, true to their youthful impulses, Xers will sidestep rules and procedures that slow them down as they push for results. They're willing to take risks and innovate—even when it drives their older bosses crazy. Given that Xers

The Real Gen X Grown-Ups

All grown up, Gen Xers are now the prime age population for nest building and child rearing at home, and maturity and leadership at work. Still self-builders, Xers have moved on domestically and will lead the way when it comes to taking care of themselves and their own. Remember, this latchkey generation was abandoned as children, and they don't want to repeat that experience with their offspring.

In fact, some of them are worried about the future of their children. As a Gen X manager for an adult group home bluntly stated: "We're dedicated to parenting. We don't want our kids to be the 'shooters.'"

The media are already giving Gen X parents high grades. Stories abound about successful Xer women who leave prestigious jobs in order start a family and remain home to raise their children. This trend has prompted many professions to rethink how to retain these talented women through such flexible work arrangements as contract work, job-sharing, and telecommuting.

Xer dads also get positive press coverage as they turn down higher-paying but more time-intensive positions to participate in child rearing. Understandably, both men and women in this generation will make family a top priority in how they structure their working lives. Unlike Schwarzkopfers and Woodstockers who defined success by where they stood on someone's corporate ladder, Xers are more aligned with Young Boomers, defining their success by their ability to create the life they want. And that life involves family, friends, hobbies, vacations—and the time to enjoy them.

compose the majority of untapped bench strength for midlevel leadership talent, managers will need to learn how to harness their innovative spirit and create customized career paths to keep this talented cohort engaged for years to come.

How to Manage Generation X

What matters most to Generation X in the workplace? What motivates them enough to stay with an organization? Whenever we pose such questions to Gen Xers, the responses point us toward seven key expectations. Your challenge as a manager, then, is to turn these into best practices.

1. Opportunities to amass marketable skills and experience
2. Career development opportunities
3. Flexible work arrangements
4. Access to coaching-style managers and wise mentors
5. Access to decision makers
6. Increasing spheres of responsibility
7. Compensation commensurate with contribution

1. Opportunities to Amass Marketable Skills and Experience

From day one, Xers knew their security lay in their own ability to amass the kind of skills and experiences that would make them valuable contributors to any workplace. Today their drive to take responsibility for their ongoing learning is shared by other generations who know job security has taken on a new meaning. Any organization that wants to attract and retain star Gen Xers—or star players of any generation, for that matter—must become known for its obsession with training.

2. Career Development Opportunities

Having a solid reputation for your commitment to training is only part of the picture: You must also be known for your investment in developing people. We make a bright line distinction between training and development. Training is the process of teaching the skills and filling the knowledge gaps necessary to successfully perform specific tasks. Everyone should receive training for every single task and responsibility assigned. Indeed, it is negligent to ask people to take on assignments without sufficient training.

Development, on the other hand, is the process of teaching transferable skills, knowledge, and wisdom. It is learning that is broadly applicable from task to task, responsibility to responsibility, role to role, and that is unlikely to become obsolete any time soon. For example, negotiating deals, delivering constructive feedback, listening actively, managing a project, motivating a team—these skills can be transferred to any setting and used at any level of any organization in any industry.

Since Generation Xers make up the plurality of prime-age workers today, they are ready for development opportunities that will advance their careers, whether it's on a technical track, a management track, or any number of professional expertise tracks you have to offer. Offering high-producing Xers opportunities to advance their careers in ways that make sense to them is a key retention strategy.

3. Flexible Work Arrangements

These include schedules, assignments, locations, and coworkers. After training in marketable skills and development opportunities, flexibility in all areas of workplace bargain is high on Gen Xers' list of must-haves.

While telecommuting and condensed schedules have gained more acceptance in many organizations, one type of flexibility is still underutilized: job-sharing. According to a recent study by the Society of Human Resource Management, only 19 percent of organizations offer job-sharing as an option. Those who do make this arrangement available report great success and higher productivity when two people bring fresh energy to a position every day. Given the family focus of new Gen X parents, this may be an excellent short-term retention strategy until they're ready to return to your workplace full time.

4. Access to Coaching-Style Managers and Wise Mentors

Generation Xers are so fiercely independent that sometimes people assume they have no interest in access to teachers and mentors at work. The truth is, most Xers place a high value on opportunities to build lasting relationships with those in the workplace who have grown wise through experience. While information and technology have usually been Xers' most reliable problem-solving resources, teachers have usually been Xers' primary human supporters outside of family. Most Xers welcome the chance to create long-term bonds of loyalty with coaching-style managers and wise mentors who can offer them the kind of learning unavailable from other sources.

5. Access to Decision Makers

Not only do Xers want to participate in decision making like Schwarzkopfers and Boomers, they also want access to the people making those decisions. Hierarchies and chains of command make no sense when workers need information, resources, or answers fast. Xers are ready to run around any interference to get what they need to get the job done—and if that means hopping over boxes on an organization chart, so be it.

6. Increasing Spheres of Responsibility

Like Boomers, Xers also want challenging work. But for Xers (and Yers as well), you'll need to add something else: increasing spheres of responsibility. Responsibility is the proving ground that you trust them, have confidence in them, and recognize their growth and development. In fact, for this cohort, increasing responsibility is what makes them feel empowered. Deprived of that empowerment, they'll walk over to your competitor.

And herein lies a dilemma. Gen Xers consistently complain that most organizational structures have a limited supply of "boxes": those up-line positions that traditionally offer increased responsibility, status, and salary. An articulate Xer in the banking industry told a roomful of Boomer executives, "It's like we're all stuck in a silo. I've been working here for three years now, and any movement up that silo is blocked by you Boomers. You're going to be around for quite a while, so what am I supposed to do? I'm ready to move now." The Boomers sat in stunned silence at the audacity of this young woman; the few Xers in the audience surreptitiously nodded their heads in agreement.

The Myth of the Organization Chart

What really happens in organizations today is typified by the case of five senior banking executives—all Boomers—whom we met at a company-wide bank meeting.

During a panel discussion, they told the audience that none of them had followed traditional leadership paths. Rather than climbing anyone's ladder, these Boomers had hopped, skipped, and jumped into new and exciting opportunities that expanded their range of influence and kept their internal fires burning. How did they do that?

- By creating reputations for going far beyond their job descriptions
- By nurturing strong ties with a kaleidoscope of mentors
- By maintaining their enthusiasm for the organization and its mission
- By remaining vigilant for the next new challenge

When new projects or positions opened, these men and women were already well known and well connected within the organization. They had developed themselves into worthy protégés of organizational allies who eagerly recommended them when senior leadership positions opened.

As a Gen Mix manager, then, teach your Gen X and Gen Y talent the importance of reputation, whether it's for their commitment to the organization or for going the extra five miles for their team. Also, let them know you will facilitate their creating a network of coaches and mentors throughout the organization who can be their allies in the future.

When options and opportunities for growth, mobility, challenge, and responsibility dry up, so does Xers' motivation. That young woman is thinking about her next career move, and if management doesn't do something quickly to retain her, she'll take her three years of training and experience to one of their competitors.

You need to understand that Xers are the perfect lateral recruiting pool and will become mid-career job switchers as they seek increased status, authority, and rewards. Many would gladly bypass more time-intensive vertical promotions if they could continue to amass marketable skills and experience with lateral moves. What this demands is nothing less than a redefinition of the traditional career paths that require climbing the ladder in a logical, sequential manner. These look neat and tidy on paper, but they're simply not the reality in many organizations.

As positions quickly go in and out of existence, as old product lines, projects, and departments fold and new ones are created, the old management-by-organization chart has ceased to have meaning.

7. Compensation Commensurate with Contribution

Grown-up Gen Xers now have to support families as well as themselves. It's no surprise, then, to learn that money is important to them, although not in a crassly materialistic sense. As a thirtysomething HR professional explained to his multigenerational colleagues, "Of course we're money-driven. Social Security is not going to be there for us and Boomers will expect us to support them in their retirement. We have families to raise, school loans to pay off, and many of us can't afford our dream homes. Believe it! Money is important to me."

The Xer Financial Forecast: Continuing Self-Reliance

The financial predicament of Xers is a serious reality and addressed in two recent, 2006 books: Tamara Draut's *Strapped: Why America's 20- and 30-Somethings Can't Get Ahead* and Anya Kamenetz's *Generation Debt: Why Now Is a Terrible Time to Be Young.* Remember, Xers were the first generation to be told they would not be as financially well off as their parents. Unfortunately, that forecast was accurate. Then, if you factor in the Social Security Administration's prediction that by 2031, when all Boomers will be past age 65, there will only be 2.1 workers for each Social Security beneficiary, you have a generation with every right to be concerned about its financial future.

True free agents to the end, Gen Xers stand in the great tradition of self-reliance—but not necessarily because they want to; they have no other choice if they want to take care of themselves and their families. As they learned from day one of their working lives, that means keeping their work options open, focusing on the short term, and constantly asking, "What's the deal around here today?" Managers who can help Xers define and achieve success on their own terms within their organizations will have access to the best talent of a generation that is already becoming our next generation of leaders.

Initiating Strategic Imperatives for Generation X

At your next managers' meeting, discuss the strategic imperatives for this generation. Which ones are so urgent that you need to tackle them immediately? What tactics do you need to implement so you are on the bleeding edge of these important Gen X issues? Be sure to address the following:

- Given the growing importance of family in their lives, what kinds of flexible work arrangements can we make available to our valuable Gen Xers?

- How do we currently identify and develop new Gen X leaders and managers in our organization? How effective is our approach?

- How could we do a better job of seizing every opportunity to develop, mentor, and coach our high potentials?

- Since Gen Xers want status, authority, and rewards, but often resist traditional management roles, how can we create new paths to leadership and redesign leadership roles that would engage their energy and talent?

Note: Since developing new leaders is so crucial to the success of any organization, we detail our practical, cost-effective approach to getting this important job done in Chapter 11.

Worksheet: How to Manage Gen Xers Today

Directions: What can you and your organization offer talented Gen Xers today so they consider you the "best deal in town"?

What Gen Xers Say They Want	What's Your "Deal" Today?
1. Opportunities to amass marketable skills and experience	
2. Career development opportunities	
3. Flexible work arrangements • Schedules • Assignments • Locations • Coworkers	
4. Access to coaching-style managers and wise mentors	
5. Access to decision makers	
6. Increasing spheres of responsibility	
7. Compensation commensurate with contribution	

Chapter 4

Generation Y:
We're Here Today!

"Of course we're an entitled generation. We grew up in an age of prosperity and got a lot from our parents. Maybe because of that, we feel an obligation to give back."

—A twentysomething government analyst

Historical Snapshot

COMING OF AGE during the most expansive economy in the twentieth century, Gen Yers are the children of Baby Boomers and the optimistic, upbeat younger siblings of Gen Xers. The first true cohort of "Global Citizens," they have been told by parents, teachers, and counselors that they can make a difference in the world, and they have already started to prove it. The most socially conscious generation since the 1960s, Yers are out in record numbers working for social causes from the environment to poverty, from local community programs to breast cancer research. Local newspapers in 2005 were filled with stories about students collecting food, clothing, and money for tsunami and hurricane victims just as they did in the aftermath of 9/11.

Combine this "giving back" impulse with Yers' facility with technology, and you have a generation on fast-forward with self-esteem. When middle and high school students collaborate with teachers on how to use technology in the curriculum (thus shaping how and what they learn), when they easily create websites and blogs to share information and make their voices heard, when they gain instant access to people and information around the world, it all adds up to a sense of empowerment that still baffles less techno-savvy adults.

Like Xers, Yers have also grown up in a scary world. Even before the events of 9/11, terrorism had already become a national phenomenon in the 90s with the Oklahoma City, World Trade Center, and Atlanta Summer Olympics bombings. School shootings in suburban and rural America exacerbated the fears that urban Xers had always carried to class with them. Designer drugs, violence-packed video games, sexually charged advertising, TV, music, and movies bombarded their everyday lives and still do. However, while the media would have you believe these young adults are hopelessly derelict, the evidence points quite clearly to the contrary. Teen arrests, pregnancies, abortions, and drunk-driving accidents are actually down. Overall, Gen Yers are doing much better than most adults realize or admit.

Influenced by education-minded Boomer parents, Gen Yers believe that education is the key to their success, and they're poised to be lifelong learners. Fueled by their facility with technology—a facility that makes even Xer skills look elementary—this "Digital Generation" is ready to learn anywhere, anytime. Add to that learning impulse Yers' ability to be great team players, and organizations have a tremendous opportunity as millions of Yers enter the workforce over the next five to 10 years.

Generation Y Goes to Work

The oldest Gen Yers entered the workplace full time at the outer edge of the boom years and expected to fulfill three ambitious goals: to find meaningful jobs within their professions of choice; to work side by side with knowledgeable, dedicated coworkers; and to earn very high salaries by the time they were 30.

Then came April 2000 and 9/11. Yers' dreams were not demolished, but they were certainly dampened by economic and global realities. Even those college graduates with solid job offers in 2001 saw those offers rescinded or put on hold. Yers suddenly found themselves facing what their Xer siblings did in the late 80s and early 90s: a tight job market or no job market at all. Many followed the path Xers had trekked a decade before. Some stayed in school to ride out the economy. Some moved back home with mom and dad to regroup. Some took lower-wage jobs outside their field to pay bills and gain experience. Fortunately, the economy is now gaining momentum. According to MonsterTrak, 72 percent of employers plan to hire 2006 college grads and 37 percent expect to recruit more entry-level candidates than they did in 2005. Things are looking up for Gen Y talent.

Generation Y at Work Today

Gen Y is the fastest-growing segment of the workforce, increasing from 14 percent in 2001 to 22 percent in 2006, and they will outnumber Gen Xers before 2011. Like Gen Xers, the most talented Yers are independent, entrepreneurial thinkers who relish responsibility, demand immediate feedback, and expect to feel a sense of accomplishment hourly. They thrive on challenging work and creative expression, love freedom and flexibility, and hate micromanagement. They're more than willing to tell you how to fix your team, department, and organization, even before they're completed your orientation program. And they'll tell you that with "attitude," an attitude which proclaims, "We're here! We're energetic, smart, creative, techno-savvy, and vocal. We're here to challenge old ideas, push forward new ideas, and use our energy to find 'work-arounds.' We're team-ready and like to collaborate. And watch out! We have very high expectations of this organization, our managers, our coworkers—and ourselves."

What Yers Expect from Your Organization

Like Xers before them, Yers are searching for organizations that have an obsession with training and development and that will offer them opportunities to amass all kinds of experiences to make them more valuable in the future. Also, like Xers, they know jobs come and go and that developing their career is their responsibility. They believe in "job security," but not in its traditional definition. According to Gen Y, "job security" means "I'll learn all I can here and as soon as opportunities to keep on learning disappear, I'll look for a better position with another organization. Of course, I'll negotiate the best deals for my expanded skills, experiences, and knowledge. I have the security of knowing I can always find a job, and I don't see that being with one company."

Every day we meet Yers who tell us, "I would have loved to stay with this company for more than a year or two, but they just didn't have anything left to offer me." Like their older siblings, Yers don't have the patience to trend water when oceans of opportunity lie before them.

Yers are also looking for employers who are not merely socially conscious, but also socially responsible; that means, organizations who respect the environment, care about their employees, create meaningful products or services, and give back to the local community. In fact, we've met Yers who tell us they are accepting lower salaries to join organizations that have a solid track record for service. For example, a 24-year-old information analyst in the federal government said he could have made $20,000 more a year in private industry, but was drawn to the public service mission of this public agency.

Finally, this "nowest" of generations demands the immediate gratification of making an immediate impact by doing meaningful work immediately. In 2005, the media covered stories of college grads who rejected high-prestige positions to work on energy issues in South America (*BusinessWeek Online,* "Welcome to the Gen Y Workforce," May 4, 2005); or to join "Teach America" so they could positively influence youth—now (*CBS Evening News,* "9/11 Grads Choose Public Service," May 24, 2005). This trend has recruiters in high-profile companies pulling their hair

We're Not a "Gen Y Workplace Experiment"

Fifty Boomer managers from public and private industry faced a panel of senior management majors at a Midwestern university. As a course assignment, these students had analyzed audience members' websites to determine how user-friendly their technology was for job seekers. They had also applied for jobs at these organizations, as well as at their competitors', to test each company's processes and response times.

After hearing the students' reports, some red-faced Boomer managers squirmed in their seats. They couldn't wait to fire questions at the seniors:

Q. What did you like or not like about the internship experience you've had at some of our organizations?

A. I didn't like being stuck in a cubicle with nothing to do. The guy that hired me hardly ever made contact with me, and my skills were never used or tested. I wanted to feel a part of the company and not like a Generation Y workplace experiment.

Q. If I hired you, how long would you stay with us before you'd leave and go elsewhere?

A. When I can offer you ways to save three million dollars and I don't get recognized for it . . . I know it's time to leave when the position is open, I have the skills to take the position, and I've been turned down. It's even worse when you have to train somebody off the street to take the job you qualify for. I hate that.

Q. What do you expect from the workplace?

A. It's not complicated. We just need an opportunity. And we don't want to be locked into a dead-end job.

Q. Where are your tattoos and body piercings?

The students laughed at the stereotype. They were all neatly dressed in business casual, having asked their professor beforehand how to dress appropriately for this meeting.

out. Just when they're ready to hire new grads again, talented Yers are looking elsewhere for opportunities to contribute to important societal issues of the day.

How to Manage Generation Y

Yers definitely have very high expectations of their managers. They claim that the quality of their relationship with their immediate manager is a critical factor in whether they stay on or leave a job. Moreover, since they typically arrive at an organization with three or four part-time jobs or internships under their belts, they are much savvier at an earlier age about what they want that relationship to look and feel like.

A twentysomething student volunteer summarized his generation's expectations when he told us, "My boss is constantly asking for our feedback on what is working and what isn't, and she actually takes our advice. The environment is comfortable, as if she were an equal. She recognizes, when things don't go right, what the problem is, and either tells us how to fix it or that it isn't in our hands to fix. She never blames everyone as a group, and most importantly, she is great at recognizing our accomplishments and hard work individually [and] as a team."

If you look at the previous description more closely, you'll find five of the major characteristics that Yers look for in a manager:

- Openness to giving and receiving feedback
- Respect for the opinions of Yers
- The interpersonal style of a colleague rather than a boss

- A pragmatic "let's fix it" attitude
- The ability to recognize individual as well as team performance

Think about the Gen Yers you manage right now. How would each of them describe his or her relationship with you? Which of your management characteristics and practices would they value? Which would they consider ineffective?

Improving your relationships with your Yers and meeting their expectations are the foundations for success with this cohort. Start building those relationships and meeting those expectations by adopting these eight best practices:

1. Get to know Yers and their individual capabilities.
2. Establish coaching relationships.
3. Treat Yers as colleagues.
4. Be flexible enough to customize schedules and assignments.
5. Consistently provide constructive feedback.
6. Tie rewards and incentives to performance only.
7. Help Yers meet their high expectations of coworkers.
8. Help Yers meet their high expectations of themselves.

1. Get to Know Yers and Their Individual Capabilities

Devote time to each Yer on your team and get to know his or her capabilities. Listen to your Yers. Ask them about their dreams and aspirations. Show them you genuinely care about their success in your organization—and in life in general. Make building those relationships as much a managerial imperative as accomplishing results. Go for a walk, take them to lunch, have coffee. Yers feel more comfortable in informal settings than in formal meetings.

2. Establish Coaching Relationships

Yers want managers who are teachers willing to help them grow and improve. Since they are the "education is cool" generation, position yourself as a dynamic source of learning. Provide resources, tools, and learning goals as needed, so that Yers progress "just-in-time." Gen Yers learn best, as most people do, when they immediately need that knowledge or skill to succeed.

3. Treat Yers as Colleagues

From day one, treat Yers like value adders, not as interns or "know-nothing kids." They can't stand condescending managers or any manager whom they cannot approach when they need questions answered. They want to feel like a colleague or an associate, not a subordinate. Treating them respectfully, and asking for respect in return, is key to a great relationship.

4. Be Flexible Enough to Customize Schedules and Assignments

Develop enough "stretch" to customize schedules and work assignments. Since some Yers are still in school, they appreciate a manager's attempts to balance work requirements with their other commitments. They also want to work faster and better than anyone else; thus you need to coach them closely by identifying goals, deadlines, and guidelines so your expectations are crystal clear. Empower them to be creative within those boundaries. In doing so, you will be offering them both the flexibility they desire and

---

Beware Parenting Your Youngest Workers . . .

Since Gen Yers have enough rule-setters, micromanagers, and stressed-out adults at home, they expect their relationship with adults at work to be more upbeat, helpful, and mutually respectful.

As one twentysomething told a roomful of Boomers: "Don't treat us at work like you treat your kids at home. Lighten up. Don't be so serious. When it comes to giving us feedback, don't harp on what already happened, on what we did wrong. Tell us how to improve."

"Tell us how to improve." Talented Gen Yers don't want overbearing parental figures at work. They want dedicated mentors and coaches who are not just willing to offer skill training, but also prepared to share the knowledge, experience, and wisdom that can shorten Yers' learning curve.

---

the security of knowing they're on track. Position the best schedules and assignments as rewards for high performance.

5. Consistently Provide Constructive Feedback

Don't wait for performance evaluations to tell Yers what they're doing right or wrong. Tell them yourself daily. Let them know what they're doing well *today;* let them know how they can improve *today.* That's what the best coaches do—observe and give immediate feedback. Avoid harping on the negative, and make it a habit to accentuate the positive. Above all, get your Yers moving ahead on the right track immediately.

6. Tie Rewards and Incentives to Performance Only

When it comes to rewards and incentives, performance should be your only guide. And don't let too much time lapse between the performance and your response to it. Make sure you deliver the praise, recognition, and rewards as soon as possible once the contribution has been made.

7. Help Yers Meet Their High Expectations of Coworkers

Yers view their colleagues as vast reservoirs of knowledge and expertise. Capitalize on that perception. Identify star employees who are experts in various competencies, and set up formal and informal mentoring and coaching opportunities. Create a database of "go to" people that Yers can easily access when they need answers to questions, strategies for handling a project, or just-in-time support and encouragement. Position every older person on your team as a teacher who has something valuable to offer young people. Tap their talents and recognize and reward their efforts in getting Yers up to speed faster and more easily.

8. Help Yers Meet Their High Expectations of Themselves

Yers want to make meaningful contributions *immediately.* This is an admirable goal, and teaching them how to reach it may take some investment of your time. The process should go smoother if you bear in mind the following:

1. Yers may be highly educated, but that doesn't mean they know the ins-and-outs of your business. (Who does at first?) Of course, you'll educate them about goals, expectations, policies, and standard operating procedures. But don't assume they know the unwritten

rules. Older managers are often surprised when they hear Yers say, "We didn't know we could [or couldn't] do that."

2. Yers are extraordinarily eager learners, but don't assume they've already learned everything. Areas that usually require teaching include:

- Work ethic. This tends to be particular to each organization, and you will have to help Yers see what it looks like in yours.

- Customer service skills. Yers will probably need to develop such skills as listening, problem solving, and handling irate people.

- Time management. Yers may need help managing their time to meet deadlines. They grew up as the most overly scheduled generation in history—with before- and after-school activities, play dates, and so forth—and some of them find self-management at work a challenge. Knowing how to break down larger goals into small benchmarks with intermediate deadlines may sound rudimentary to you—but it won't to them.

Be sure to make work ethic, customer service skills, and time management skills the focus of Gen Yers' initial training.

There's no denying it: This is high-maintenance work and Gen Yers are the highest-maintenance workforce in history. They want training now. They want feedback now. They want recognition now. They want to make an impact now.

Work Ethic: It Has to Be Taught

One of our star Gen Y colleagues enlightened us about work ethic. At age 16, she took "the job that many people say they never will do." She went to work at McDonald's. For two and a half years, this vegetarian wore the smell of fast-food grease in her hair and on her clothes. But, she recounts, those years taught her basic lessons in work ethic, pride, and self-discipline that have served her well in her professional life ever since.

"It was at McDonald's," she said, "that I would always hear the phrase, 'If you have time to lean, you have time to clean.' The job is never done and there is always something that can be improved. This opened my eyes to the fact that work ethic is not a born trait and must sometimes be taught."

This Gen Yer learned this lesson well: Her own pride, self-discipline, and work ethic have already earned her several high-visibility management positions in the hospitality industry.

Another case in point. A fortysomething nurse manager told us about a newly hired Gen Y nurse who excelled at her job. The only problem was, when she completed her workload, she sat down. She had no idea that the hospital culture required her to look for opportunities to help her colleagues. Her manager realized, "If this were a Boomer, I would have said she was lazy. But this was a young nurse who just didn't know. As soon as I coached her, she responded enthusiastically. She wasn't lazy. She just didn't know how we work around here."

What does a good, solid "work ethic" look like in your organization? How are you making it clear to your Gen Yers that this is "how we work around here"?

They want to change everything now. However, if you're willing to do this high-maintenance work, you can turn these exciting young workers into the highest producers in history. Yers are already becoming a very resourceful, productive part of the workforce.

In fact, every day we meet mature Yers already in management positions who are running circles around their older colleagues. They have the energy, enthusiasm, and "can do" attitude that can re-ignite a team. Not encumbered by the attitudes and values of the workplace of the past, they're making the extra effort to challenge old policies and procedures, to drive initiative, and to push your organization into the workplace of the future. If you can develop their talent and focus their energy, you'll have a strategic advantage over your competitors as 10 million more Yers enter the workforce in the next five years.

Initiating Strategic Imperatives for Generation Y

At your next managers' meeting, discuss the strategic imperatives for this cohort. Which ones are so urgent that you need to tackle them immediately? What tactics do you need to implement so you are on the bleeding edge of these important Gen Y issues? Be sure to discuss the following:

- How effective is our current orientation program in engaging the enthusiasm and energy of our new recruits from day one? How can we create a program that gets them up to speed faster and has them making important contributions sooner?

- Are our managers trained to coach younger workers every step of the way on every single thing that's essential to their positions, from work ethic to time management to customer service? If not, how will we get them up to speed?

- How can we engage our current Gen Y stars in becoming peer leaders who can help with the transition of young new hires into our work environment and culture, making it more fun and productive?

- How can we identify star teachers of all ages throughout our organization who are ready and willing to participate in shaping the youngest workforce? How can we communicate their areas of expertise and availability to Gen Yers?

- How do we offer our Gen Yers a continuous sense of ownership of their tasks and an increasing sense of responsibility so they know we trust them?

- How will we help Gen Yers meet their high expectations of our organization, their managers, coworkers, and themselves?

Self-Evaluation: How to Manage Generation Y

Directions: Evaluate yourself on each of the Gen Y expectations below. How well are you doing right now? How can you improve in the future as you build solid working relationships with each member of this young workforce?

1. Get to know Yers and their individual capabilities.

2. Establish coaching relationships.

3. Treat Yers as colleagues.

4. Be flexible enough to customize schedules and assignments.

5. Consistently provide constructive feedback.

6. Tie rewards and incentives to performance only.

7. Help Yers meet their high expectations of coworkers.

8. Help Yers meet their high expectations of themselves.

Worksheet: Who's in Your Generation Mix?

Directions: Think about the Schwarzkopfers, Woodstockers, Young Boomers, Gen Xers, and Gen Yers you manage. Create a form like the one below and list your employees according to their generation. How do they exemplify the experiences, attitudes, behaviors, and expectations of their generation? What challenges do they provide you with right now?

After you finish reading this book, come back to your list and ask yourself: How will I address these challenges to become a more effective Gen Mix manager?

Generation	Experiences, Attitudes, Behaviors, Expectations	Challenges
Schwarzkopfers		
Woodstockers		
Young Boomers		
Gen X		
Gen Y		

Overview: Managing Your Generation Mix

Schwarzkopfers (before 1946)

Management Best Practices

1. Ask about the work itself—and offer learning experiences. Have a one-on-one conversation about job satisfaction with each Schwarzkopfer.

2. Make it clear: no "coasting" allowed. Rigorously offer feedback and base rewards solely on performance.

3. Address the new standard of customization. Engage Schwarzkopfers in updating standard operating procedures (SOPs) to be used for future training.

4. Encourage "making the call." Support these experienced people in using their own judgment to make business decisions.

5. Create knowledge transfer programs.

   - Create a "go-to" list of Schwarzkopfer experts whom younger workers can contact when they need immediate information on a customer, client, process, project, or procedure.

   - Establish teams of Schwarzkopfers who do similar work, and engage them in generating answers to the most frequently asked questions they receive about the organization's products, services, or policies.

   - Bring together Schwarzkopfers who have experience handling difficult customers, and engage them in creating real-life scripts that others can use for training purposes.

   - Engage Schwarzkopfers in coaching new hires on how to get up to speed more quickly.

   - Formalize job shadowing and job-sharing opportunities so younger workers can experience the work Schwarzkopfers do up-close and personal. ➡

Overview: Managing Your Generation Mix
(continued)

➡️ **Schwarzkopfers (before 1946)**

- Engage interested Schwarzkopfers in becoming trainers of the skill sets they have mastered.

- Ask Schwarzkopfers how they want to be recognized and rewarded for their contributions to your knowledge transfer program.

Initiating Strategic Imperatives

- What negative stereotypes does our organization hold about Schwarzkopfers? How are we going to dispel those stereotypes by supporting the "truths" about this generation? How are we going to make this an age-friendly workplace for this generation?

- How much does our organization value and rely upon the experience of our older workers? When things go wrong, to whom do we turn to get things back on track? How do we publicly acknowledge and reward our Schwarzkopfers for their expertise?

- We need to begin the process of capturing and transferring the knowledge, skill, and wisdom of older workers immediately. How will we do that? How will we recognize and reward them for their contributions to the process?

- We need to redefine retirement and create flexible work programs so older workers will want to keep working for us. What would those programs look like? Which can we offer right now to Schwarzkopfers who are nearing retirement?

➡️

Overview: Managing Your Generation Mix
(continued)

Baby Boomers (1946–1964)

Management Best Practices

1. Honor their historical memory. Like Schwarzkopfers, Boomers can put a contextual spin on why certain policies and procedures are non-negotiable and why certain approaches or innovations just won't work.

2. Give them recognition. This means honoring their opinions, skills, knowledge, potential, and contributions and finding appropriate ways to reward them.

3. Let them try out new ideas. Offer them the flexibility and authority to experiment, and support them if they fail.

4. Help bridge the team-individual divide. Many Boomers are driven by conflicting impulses between doing what's best for the team and distinguishing themselves. Help them address that conflict in a way that benefits both.

5. Coach and challenge. Become a coach who facilitates goals, not dictates them, and who challenges Boomers to grow. Remember: Self-improvement is a major Boomer aspiration. Challenge them to mentor the next generation of leaders and workers.

In general, remember that Boomers want to be seen and treated as individuals. They value creating personal relationships and building rapport. Spend time getting to know them individually and divest yourself of the assumptions you have about people in their forties, fifties, and early sixties.

➥

Overview: Managing Your Generation Mix
(continued)

➡ **Baby Boomers (1946–1964)**

Initiating Strategic Imperatives

- How can we make our workplace age-friendly for people in their forties, fifties, and sixties?

- How much does our organization value and rely upon the experience of our Boomer workers? How do we publicly acknowledge and reward our Boomers for their expertise?

- We need to identify talented Boomer workers who are nearing retirement. How can we help them redefine retirement so their skills and talents stay with us for as long as possible? How do we include them in succession planning and knowledge transfer?

- Which older Boomers in our organization hold leadership positions? How do we encourage them to identify and develop high-potential employees so there will be enough bench strength to take over leadership roles as they retire? How we will recognize and reward these current leaders for their development skills?

➡

Overview: Managing Your Generation Mix
(continued)

Generation X (1965–1977)

Management Best Practices

Give Gen Xers what matters most to them in the workplace by meeting their seven key expectations:

1. Opportunities to amass marketable skills and experience. Such skills and experience mean security to Xers, who prefer organizations known for an obsession with training.

2. Career development opportunities. It's also important that your organization is known for its investment in developing people.

3. Flexible work arrangements. These include flexible schedules, assignments, locations, and coworkers.

4. Access to coaching-style managers and wise mentors. Most Xers place high value on opportunities to build lasting relationships with such people in the workplace.

5. Access to decision makers. When in need, Xers want to get information, resources, and answers quickly.

6. Increasing spheres of responsibility. For Xers, increasing responsibility is what makes them feel empowered.

7. Compensation commensurate with contribution. This has become especially important to Xers because they now have families to support as well as themselves.

Overview: Managing Your Generation Mix
(continued)

➡ **Generation X (1965–1977)**

Initiating Strategic Imperatives

- Given the growing importance of family in their lives, what kinds of flexible work arrangements can we make available to our valuable Gen Xers?

- How do we currently identify and develop new Gen X leaders and managers in our organization? How effective is our approach?

- How could we do a better job of seizing every opportunity to develop, mentor, and coach our high potentials?

- Since Gen Xers want status, authority, and rewards, but often resist traditional management roles, how can we create new paths to leadership and redesign leadership roles that would engage their energy and talent?

➡

Overview: Managing Your Generation Mix
(continued)

Generation Y (1978–1989)

Management Best Practices

1. Get to know Yers and their individual capabilities. Show Yers you genuinely care about their success in your organization—and in life in general.

2. Establish coaching relationships. Position yourself as a dynamic source of learning, providing resources, tools, and learning goals as needed.

3. Treat Yers as colleagues. Yers want to be regarded as value adders, not as "know-nothing kids."

4. Be flexible enough to customize schedules and assignments. Position the best schedules and assignments as rewards for high performance.

5. Consistently provide constructive feedback. Let Yers know what they're doing well *today,* and how they can improve *today.*

6. Tie rewards and incentives to performance only. Don't wait to deliver praise, recognition, and rewards for good performance; do it as soon as possible once the performance has been demonstrated.

7. Help Yers meet their high expectations of coworkers. Position every older person on your team as a teacher with something valuable to offer Yers.

8. Help Yers meet their high expectations of themselves. Be sure to make work ethic, customer service skills, and time management skills the focus of Yers' initial training.

➡

Overview: Managing Your Generation Mix
(concluded)

➡ Generation Y (1978–1989)

Initiating Strategic Imperatives

- How effective is our current orientation program in engaging the enthusiasm and energy of our new recruits from day one? How can we create a program that gets them up to speed faster and has them making important contributions sooner?

- Are our managers trained to coach younger workers every step of the way on every single thing that's essential to their positions, from work ethic to time management to customer service? If not, how will we get them up to speed?

- How can we engage our current Gen Y stars in becoming peer leaders who can help with the transition of young new hires into our work environment and culture, making it more fun and productive?

- How can we identify star teachers of all ages throughout our organization who are ready and willing to participate in shaping the youngest workforce? How can we communicate their areas of expertise and availability to Gen Yers?

- How do we offer our Gen Yers a continuous sense of ownership of their tasks and an increasing sense of responsibility so they know we trust them?

- How will we help Gen Yers meet their high expectations of our organization, their managers, coworkers, and themselves?

Chapter 5.

Bridging the Generational (Mis)Understanding Gap

READING ABOUT GENERATIONAL DIVERSITY is one thing; engaging team members in a lively discussion of cross-generational issues is another. One of the most effective ways we've found to facilitate such discussion is by conducting a training exercise we call "Bridging the Generational (Mis)Understanding Gap." This activity takes 2 to 3 hours to complete, and will help the members of each generation do the following:

- Create a profile of their generation's characteristics, values, and contributions to the organization

- Share their perceptions of the characteristics, values, and contributions of other generations

- Validate the uniqueness of all generations and the contributions each makes to the team

- Raise awareness of what each generation can learn from and teach others

Now let's take a close look at how to conduct this effective exercise.

Conducting the Exercise

☞ Getting Started

Invite your team to an informal meeting to discuss generational diversity. Assure them that this is not a conflict-resolution session but, rather, an opportunity to share insights and understanding about age-related issues. The purpose is to clear up any misunderstandings that block more productive relationships. Create a comfortable environment, one that's conducive to fun, and, if appropriate, provide refreshments. Keep the tone light and upbeat.

The only "equipment" you'll need for this exercise are flipcharts and markers for each discussion group and copies of the worksheets provided in this chapter. The meeting room should be set up with tables, preferably round, and have enough elbow room so people can take notes and comfortably engage in conversation.

☞ Step 1. Topic Introduction and Group Preparation

Distribute worksheets and introduce the concept of generational diversity. Define the generations demographically, and say a few words about their history and their role in the workplace. (See Chapters 1 to 4). Spend no more than 20 minutes on your opening remarks.

Ask participants to identify themselves by generation; then, break them into discussion groups accordingly. If there are more than eight representatives of any generation, divide the larger group into smaller groups.

Ask each group to appoint—or get volunteers for— these functional roles:

1. A team leader to keep the discussion on track and ensure that everyone has the opportunity to participate

2. A note taker to record the team's findings on a flipchart

3. A timekeeper to clock the exercises

4. A reporter to articulate discussion points to the room at large

☞ Step 2. Creating Generational Profiles

Once the teams are ready, describe what you'd like them to accomplish using the "Worksheet 1" handout. Be sure to include these directions:

- Team leaders will facilitate a discussion of the characteristics, values, and contributions of their own generation.

- All note takers will use the same format for their notes. They should write their generation's name at the top of the flipchart page, and then create three columns headed Characteristics, Values, and Contributions.

- Timekeepers should clock this exercise at 12 minutes. This includes both the discussion and flipchart preparation.

- Teams should not share their findings, including flipchart notes, until you direct them to.

Let reporters know they will have 5 to 7 minutes to explain their team's insights later in the program.

Bridging the Generational (Mis)Understanding Gap: Worksheet 1

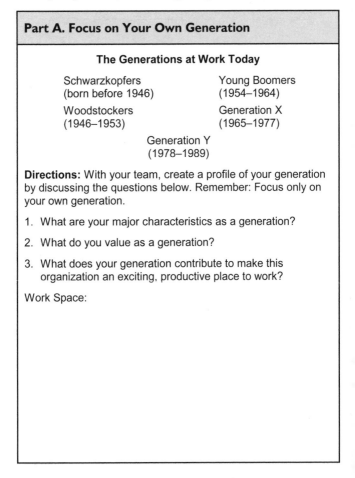

Part A. Focus on Your Own Generation

The Generations at Work Today

Schwarzkopfers
(born before 1946)

Young Boomers
(1954–1964)

Woodstockers
(1946–1953)

Generation X
(1965–1977)

Generation Y
(1978–1989)

Directions: With your team, create a profile of your generation by discussing the questions below. Remember: Focus only on your own generation.

1. What are your major characteristics as a generation?

2. What do you value as a generation?

3. What does your generation contribute to make this organization an exciting, productive place to work?

Work Space:

Now ask the teams to begin the activity. When their 12 minutes is up, ensure that all team discussions have been completed. If not, allow another minute or two for a wrap-up. Then, without providing any feedback, move on to the next step.

☞ Step 3. Perceiving Other Generations

Teams will only need a team leader and a timekeeper for this section.

Ask leaders to use Worksheet 2 to facilitate a discussion of their own group's perceptions of other generations. What are the characteristics and values of those generations? What can their own generation learn from and teach others? (Note: Keep the discussion to generations that are actually represented by teams.)

Direct timekeepers to clock this activity at 12 minutes, and instruct everyone to take their own notes on the worksheet.

Now ask the teams to begin the activity. When their 12 minutes is up, ensure that all team discussions have been completed. If not, allow another minute or two for a wrap-up. Then, move on to the next step.

☞ Step 4. Sharing, Discussion, and Challenges

Each team should now display their flipcharts from Step 1 so that everyone can see them. Beginning with Gen Y, and moving from them to the older groups in turn, facilitate this two-part process for each generation:

Bridging the Generational (Mis)Understanding Gap: Worksheet 2

Part B. Focus on Other Generations

Directions: With your team, focus on each generation other than yours and discuss the questions below.

1. What are the characteristics of this generation?

2. What are the values of this generation?

3. What can you learn from this generation?

4. What can you teach this generation?

	Characteristics	Values	Learn	Teach
Schwarzkopfers				
Woodstockers				
Young Boomers				
Generation X				
Generation Y				

1. Give each reporter 5 to 7 minutes to present his or her generation's characteristics, values, and contributions.

2. Give the other groups 10 to 12 minutes to ask questions, make comments, and share what their own generation can learn from, as well as teach, this generation.

After the reports and discussions are completed, ask participants: What did you learn about other generations that you didn't expect to learn?

Emphasize this point: *Our task is to acknowledge and honor our differences and to focus on our strengths. We want to leverage both differences and strengths to maximize the learning, productivity, and innovation of our team. And we want to capitalize on learning from and teaching one another.*

Finally, pose this challenge: *What can we do to make this organization* [or department or team] *an age-friendly environment for people of all generations?*

Ask participants to bring suggestions to the next meeting as part of the follow-up to this activity. Reemphasize: *If we are going to create a collaborative team that gets the best work done every day, our task is to maximize the talents, skills, and contributions of each person on this team. We respect and honor our differences and use them as springboards to learning, productivity, and innovation.*

What We've Learned . . .

As trainers, we've been consistently gratified by the quality of insight and information, respect and appreciation, that emerges during this discussion. Here are some highlights of what we've heard from hundreds of participants. Expect some of these same themes to surface during your team exercise.

Focus on Gen Y

Since they're the new kids on the block and, in most cases, haven't had the opportunity to engage in this kind of open exchange with their colleagues, Gen Yers usually get the most attention. Older generations are frequently interested in knowing three things about them: How they want to be managed, why they feel so entitled, and what they mean when they say they want respect.

The Yers we've met have been very vocal in their responses—in fact, they're often the most outspoken of all the generations. They tell their older colleagues they're constantly looking for "work-arounds" and often don't know the background history that makes current policies and procedures necessary. Without that knowledge, their perception is limited to "These older people are entrenched in old ways of doing things. They don't want to change."

Older managers learn they can't assume that Yers know the historical context of anything, or that this cohort will do as they're told without knowing why they should do it. Rather than taking offense at Yer "push-backs," managers realize, it's possible to use those challenges as an opportunity (1) to re-examine "the way we do things around here"

A Lesson on "What's in It for Me?"

When during this exercise a Gen X HR professional confronted her Gen Y colleagues about what she perceived as their self-centered sense of entitlement, she was in for a reality check. The fiftysomething corporate vice president of Human Resources stood up and confronted the Xer in return. "And what about all the times you've come to me with 'I need this, I want that'? Isn't that right?" she asked.

The VP received a begrudging affirmative from the thirty-something Gen Xer, and then turned to her multigenerational staff. "In fact, you've all done it," she told them. "Remember who I am; I know all of you! And if you don't tell me what you need and want to be successful here, I can't do my job. All of you need to have a healthy dose of WIIFM. That's not a bad thing."

---

to make updates, and (2) to tap the energy and innovative spirit of young workers who may have some fresh approaches to old processes.

Conversely, Yers tell their older colleagues they need to learn patience and persistence. They're often unaware that "Don't just do something, stand there" may be the best strategy when answers to problems aren't clear. As older managers assure Yers, "Faster is not always better or smarter."

Focus on Gen X

Gen X has arrived. They proudly tell other generations about their strong work ethic, their ability to use technology to streamline processes, and their flexible, innovative, risk-taking spirits that make them valuable to their organizations. Like Woodstockers, they care about issues such as the environment, crime, and social equality. Like Young Boomers, they demand work/life balance.

Older managers often want to know if Xers feel left out or overlooked now that Gen Yers seem to be getting all the attention. These independent, ambitious "go-getters" seem amused by the question; they've always been accustomed to taking care of themselves. Now they are confident enough in their experience and contributions not to let themselves be overlooked. Not obsessed with climbing the corporate ladder, these free agents are as energetic, creative, and adaptable as ever as they make lifestyle choices that contribute to their happiness and health. Since they have a solid track record of valuable contributions to an organization, and they are seen as the next generation of leaders, Xers proclaim themselves change agents who bridge the values gap between older and younger generations.

Focus on Young Boomers

This cohort breathes a collective sigh of relief when they hear that we don't place them in the Age of Aquarius. They've always felt disconnected from their older Boomer colleagues, but haven't known precisely what that meant. For the first time, they have the opportunity to define themselves, and they energetically seize it.

Like Woodstockers and Xers, Young Boomers claim to bridge the older and younger workforces. As one manager explained, "We bring both an understanding of future goals and the experience of the past 25-plus years to a developing workplace. We are a bridge between the soon-to-retire owners and operators and the still-inexperienced younger workers."

In contrast to Xers' strong suspicions about organizations, these Young Boomers see themselves as cautiously loyal and much more realistic about life and work than the idealistic Woodstockers. They're proud of their strong work ethic, dependability, commitment, knowledge, and experience. They claim they are rarely out sick, are not only willing to take on additional work but actively seek it, and want to mentor others.

They also see themselves as empathetic supervisors and coworkers who are dedicated to their jobs and take pride in doing them well.

Finally, they also realize that unless they gain a voice for themselves distinct from their older siblings, no magazine will cover their sixtieth birthday in the year 2014.

Focus on the Woodstock Generation

When the Woodstock generation starts to reminisce about their "Turn on, tune in, drop out" days, Xers and Yers usually sit there drop-jawed. These older professionals suddenly seem to be wearing bell-bottoms and tie-dyed shirts, holding hands, and singing, "All we are saying is give peace a chance."

Proud of their social rebellion and open about the "hits" and "trips" they took in the 60s and 70s, they still proclaim, "We are cool!" As a fiftysomething administrator in a police department said, "We made a positive change. We questioned assumptions. We liberated society for the arts, movies, women, and people of color."

Woodstockers also admit they're still competitive and self-centered, but have a strong commitment to the mission of their organizations. Now they add "family" to the list of values from their youth: peace, love, and freedom. Many older Boomer work addicts have learned from their own adult children and younger colleagues that there's much more to life than work. And that some of the time, at least, work should be fun.

Interestingly, Woodstockers' perceptions of themselves are often at odds with those other generations. While these Boomers see themselves as creative mold-breakers who are willing to experiment, younger generations see them as stuck in the rut. While they pride themselves on being great change leaders, others see them as holding on to the status quo.

In the course of discussion, both sides usually meet in the middle: Boomers explain the "why" of when, where, and how they must hold the line (their institutional memory and years of experience give them credibility); younger generations feel the frustration these seasoned pros have experienced while trying to move often stodgy organizational cultures into the twenty-first century. It's a reality check for all generations.

Focus on the Schwarzkopf Generation

Most Schwarzkopfers see their strengths as loyalty, dependability, responsibility, altruism, and a strong work ethic. They are proud of their accomplishments and their commitment to their organizations. Other generations agree that they can count on these seasoned workers for everything from providing historical perspective to producing an important document. As one Xer said, "They're pack rats, all right. I needed a 1995 memo and Marge had it on file. She knew just where it was just-in-time. I really appreciated that."

Other generations usually express a sense of gratitude to this generation, many of whom have dedicated over 30 years to an organization. As one senior manager, listening to this conversation, said, "I'm sitting here trying to figure out how I can keep you from retiring! You are valuable to all of us."

Walking on Common Ground

As they listen to each other, members of multigenerational teams find that under the strata of age diversity lies a bedrock of unifying needs and expectations. For example, a fiftysomething insurance agent was amazed to learn that younger employees want the same things he does: respect, creative challenges, the opportunity to add value, increasing responsibility, recognition for their contributions, and flexibility. The only difference, he realized, is that they want, expect, and demand these at the beginning of their careers. They know it no other way. Now, toward the end of his career, he finally realizes that he can have what matters most to him by becoming a free agent and negotiating for them. He and members of every generation in today's workplace are responsible for their careers, lives, and families; and, as part of the workplace bargain, they must develop a healthy sense of WIIFM as they contribute the best work alongside the best people of all ages every day.

The Next Step

This multigenerational training activity will be an eye-opener for you and your team. It isn't a panacea for all future misunderstandings, but it will start to clear the air and help each generation acknowledge the strengths and contributions each makes to the workplace. While this exercise is an important first step, it is only the beginning. If you stop here, you're left with "Now that we understand one another, let's be polite, show gratitude, and make nice." That works—as it does for all diversity issues—but only to a point.

The next step is to steer your team toward the finish line: the highest-quality results achieved collaboratively in record time by the best people. Age is no longer an issue; the willingness and ability of team members to leverage their strengths and their contributions is. How do you do that? Take a look at Part Two.

PART TWO
What Does It Take to Become a Great Gen Mix Manager?

What You Can Expect

IF YOU'RE LIKE MOST MANAGERS WE MEET, you find yourself caught in a daily tug-of-war. On one side is your manager who puts pressure on you to get more work out of fewer people using fewer resources; on the other side is your team who puts pressure on you to relieve the pressure. Both sides have needs and expectations the other doesn't want to hear about. As the person in the middle, you're expected to win the war, relieve the stress, and produce great results. To do that, you need to master three basic skill sets: focus, communication, and customization.

1. **Focus.** You must zero in with laser-like precision on the mission and goals of your organization and team, helping members clearly define how their talents, skills, and expertise make an impact on each.

2. **Communication.** You must create easy-to-use communications systems that provide information and resources to each person just-in-time, all the time.

3. **Customization.** Finally, you must keep team members energized and engaged in doing their work better, faster, safer, and more cost-effectively

by customizing incentives that recognize, reward, and drive high performance. One-size-fits-all is out when you're managing an age-diverse team. Customization becomes your key to motivating and retaining talent.

This section offers you 25 best practices that the best Gen Mix managers use to master these skills, and provides you with exercises for implementing those best practices with your team.

Chapter 6

Focus:
It's All About the Work

THINK ABOUT IT: The reason you hire people in the first place is to get the best work done every day. Work is all about "the work," and "the work" is the solid common ground on which people of all ages walk. For today's diverse workforce, that work needs to be meaningful, challenging, and varied; it needs to offer everyone opportunities for growth, learning, recognition, and reward. Remember, Schwarzkopfers claim that work motivates them when it's satisfying; Boomers derive their identity from it and want to be respected for it; Xers find their security in amassing skills from it; Yers want to make a difference through it. And, every generation today is trying to balance it with their personal lives.

Your job as a Gen Mix manager is twofold:

1. To ensure that everyone understands that "the work" is what unites them and that collaborating to get lots of great work done every day is why they're here

2. To help everyone understand that talented people of every age are unwilling to contribute their creativity to directionless organizations or teams where they produce less value and receive less credit

The first skill set you must master, then, is a laser-like focus on what "great work" means. This competency is especially important in today's fast-paced world, where change is the norm, projects come and go rapidly, and people are deployed on one set of tasks today and another set tomorrow. It requires that you constantly cut through the non-essentials and focus everyone of all ages on the mission, goals, roles, and responsibilities inherent in "the work."

This chapter provides you with seven "best practices" for establishing and maintaining that laser focus. Practices 1 to 5 are essential focusing steps that should be done in the order we describe. Practices 6 and 7 can be done at your discretion when your team is ready to move to the next level of collaboration.

The Essential Focusing Steps

Best Practice 1: Light the "Fire in the Belly"

Why Are We Here?

One of your challenges as a manager is to keep the motivational fires burning in the bellies of every direct report. How? By focusing on the meaning and purpose of the work you ask them to do every day. The classic complaint that employees of all ages have had about their managers is "We don't know why we're doing what we're doing. And we certainly don't know where our roles and responsibilities begin and end."

Remember, Gen Yers are constantly asking "Why?" about everything you ask them to do, and Gen Xers get impatient when time is wasted on seemingly meaningless tasks.

Therefore, investing time to make the mission of your organization and your team the compelling answer to "Why are we here?" cuts through many of their complaints.

The "Fire" of Your Mission

Vision is about the future, but mission is all about right now. If your organization has a mission statement, pull it out and engage your team members in a lively discussion about the purpose and values that drive the work they do today. Use the historical memory of your Schwarzkopfers and Woodstockers to provide the backdrop for this discussion. At least some of them will be able to offer the rationale for the mission's direction and language. If your organization doesn't have a mission statement—or if it's so outdated as to be meaningless—seize the opportunity to create one collaboratively.

During your team discussion, focus on the mission and ask your team to address the following questions:

- Is our organization's mission still compelling enough to motivate us to do our best work every day? If not, why not? What would it take to compel us to contribute our talents and creative energy every day?

- Has the mission dramatically changed over time? Does it need revision to get us in sync with marketplace realities?

- How can we redefine the mission so we can really buy into it?

- Are we aligned with its values? If not, why not? What would it take to achieve alignment?

Use your team's answers to these question re-ignite everyone's commitment.

Best Practice 2: Define Your Team/Project Mission

Missions Within the Mission

Each team, each project, each committee also has its own mission. Every time people begin working together as a group, invite them to define why their group exists and how its purpose aligns with the organization's mission. Make sure they know how their accountabilities—from goals and deadlines to important decisions to resource allocations—fit within a broader context. Ask them:

• How will this goal, decision, or resource further our team's (or project's, or committee's) mission?

• How does this support our organization's mission?

If there is no positive response, don't just move on to something else: Stand there until the group's direction is clear. Mapping out the direction at the beginning of a process will eliminate time wasted retracing steps down the line.

Defining Your Team/Project Mission

Ask team members to participate in a brainstorming session to clarify their present mission or that of their next project. Use the following questions as guidelines, and work toward consensus.

• Why does our team/project exist?

• What do we do that no one else can do? What will the team/project accomplish?

- What makes our team/project special?

- What would the organization lose if our team/project disappeared?

Once the team has defined its mission, ensure that each member has a copy of the mission statement and that a copy is posted where everyone on the team can see it.

Don't underestimate the power of "pride of affiliation": the bragging rights that come along with being part of a great team that has a great mission with a great track record doing great work with great people.

Best Practice 3: Clarify the Team's Work

What's the Work?

Once the team has defined its mission, the focus turns to the work. The team must now clarify such things as its goals, tasks, deadlines, and guidelines.

Clarifying the Team's Work

☞ **Step 1**

Facilitate your team's discussion of these important questions:

- What work needs to be done by this team—or on this project? (Ensure that older employees who have worked on similar teams or projects share their experience and wisdom.)

- What projects, tasks, and responsibilities must be accomplished?

- For each project, task, and responsibility, what are the major goals and deadlines?

- What are the key guidelines that must be observed in order for us to meet those goals and deadlines?

- Which guidelines are non-negotiable? Which can be scrutinized for "work-arounds"?

Be sure that younger employees understand that "non-negotiable" doesn't mean "We're doing this because we've always done it this way before." Rather, enlighten them about the repercussions of roaming outside the parameters. Also, be sure everyone is open to new approaches to those guidelines. Some guidelines may be streamlined, changed, or eliminated to achieve better results.

Create a form like the "Scope of Our Work" template on the next page, and use it to document your discussion.

☞ Step 2

Once everyone is clear about the team's work, decide who will continue as a member and who will not. During the course of these discussions, you'll soon discover that certain members now feel unable or unwilling to commit themselves to your team. Some may be unaccustomed to being held to such clear-cut, concrete accountabilities; others may realize they lack the skills or expertise to contribute to the team's work at the required level. Whatever the reason, be prepared to remove such people from your team. They may be more effective on another team or in another department; or they may need more training or outplacement counseling.

The Scope of Our Work

Projects, Tasks, and Responsibilities	Goals and Deadlines	Guidelines: Non-Negotiable/ Negotiable?	Legitimate/ Helpful Work-Arounds

Every player on your team must be assured that he or she is working with committed, enthusiastic contributors. Remember, Schwarzkopfers want to respect the people they work with, Boomers pride themselves on effective teamwork, and Gen Yers have very high expectations of their colleagues. We've discovered that when everyone knows that others are willing to add value, contribute 100 percent, and pull their weight to get the best work done, age is never a problem. It's an opportunity to share expertise and learn more quickly.

☞ Step 3

Before a project begins, ask team members to discuss how progress will be benchmarked and how success will be defined. How will they measure individual contributions as well as those of the team as a whole? How much "tolerance for mistakes" will the team allow in order to reach the best solutions? How much time for "trial and error" must be factored into deadlines?

To stay ahead of your competition, your team must be willing to innovate and take risks. Consequently, old methods of measuring success may not work at all in today's unpredictable marketplace, and may even be counterproductive. We've discovered that the people doing the work often have the best insight into how to evaluate their work. Engage everyone in creating that process.

Best Practice 4: Define Each Team Member's Mission

Who's on First?

Once you know who's remaining on your team, clarify each member's personal mission: his or her role or function on the team. Few things destroy a team faster than a manager not helping players define their roles or players not understanding those roles.

Defining Each Member's Mission

Ask your team members to answer these questions:

- What resources of time, energy, skills, knowledge, and talents will each of us contribute to the team effort?

- How will we collaborate to get the work done?

- Who is best suited to do what? By when?

- How flexible is each team player in terms of learning new skills, implementing new strategies, and changing direction when necessary?

- What starring roles and what supporting roles is each person willing to play?

Successful sports franchises demand individual excellence, no matter what role an athlete plays. When called upon, a bench player needs to contribute 100 percent as readily as a starter. In fact, the most successful teams have "deep" benches as well as stars who can assist as well as score, who can follow as well as lead. Team members who can successfully function in a variety of roles become your most valuable "utility" players, offering the team the flexibility it needs to seize new opportunities or change strategies quickly. The best Gen Mix managers, then, are constantly building bench strength, particularly with younger workers.

Best Practice 5:
Maximize Everyone's Uniqueness NOW!

Too many team members—especially those new to the organization—have no idea of the great breadth and depth of knowledge and experience their coworkers bring to work each day. One way to get that information out on the table is to dedicate a staff meeting to a round-robin discussion of the talents, skills, and expertise your team can leverage immediately. Not only will everyone become aware of the powerhouse of talent they have surrounding them, but they'll also learn who's available for formal or informal coaching opportunities.

We've conducted the exercise on the next page during our multigenerational workshops, and whether the audience has been filled with white-collar, blue-collar, or no-collar participants, the results have been extraordinary. Try it out at your next staff meeting.

During the second step of this exercise, we've observed that some people are unaware of the positive impact they've had on others. When they receive praise and appreciation for contributions they've overlooked or thought too insignificant, their value is affirmed and their commitment to continue making contributions is strengthened.

Also, the positive, supportive environment that this initial discussion creates makes it easier for everyone to discuss their responses to the second and third topics: the area(s) they want to work on for improvement, and how and where they can get the training, coaching, or mentoring they need.

❖ Exercise: Optimizing Uniqueness

1. Give team members a handout listing the following three questions:

   - What do I have to offer the team in terms of experience, talents, skills, knowledge?

   - What is the one area I want to improve on during the next quarter?

   - I'd like support in terms of coaching, training, and mentoring. What can other team members offer me? What other resources outside the team are available?

   Allow members 5 minutes or so to think about their responses and take their own notes.

2. Now call the team to attention and ask someone to volunteer to share his or her responses to the first question. Assure members that everyone will have equal air time during this exercise. Ask them to listen carefully to their colleague and then to offer feedback based on the following:

   - Specific examples of how this individual has used his or her experience, talents, skills, and knowledge to make this a better team

   - What other, unmentioned contributions this individual has made to help the team achieve its mission and goals

3. Stay focused on the same volunteer and ask for his or her responses to the other two questions, on improvement and resources. Again, ask for team feedback.

4. Repeat this process until all team members have had a chance to share responses and receive feedback.

During the third step, we've observed that seasoned team members with expertise in that person's needed areas often offer to create learning partnerships to bring the person up to speed. Or, if they know of great coaches or trainers outside the team, they make recommendations and facilitate forging connections. Either way, the individual in the spotlight is left with specific resources for furthering his or her development on the team.

For Schwarzkopfers who say their coworkers give meaning to their jobs, for Boomers who want respect for contributions, for Xers who are always on the lookout to learn new skills, and for Yers who consider their colleagues huge reservoirs of learning, this discussion is particularly engaging and meaningful. *Everyone* benefits.

Revisit this exercise quarterly to update the team on performance improvements. Morale and productivity soar when members realize everyone is committed to becoming more and more valuable team players.

Moving to the Next Level of Collaboration

Best Practice 6: Create Learn-Teach Plans

When team members of all ages are comfortable enough with one another to admit, "I need some help in this area," or, "I have expertise I'd be happy to share," you've created an environment where learning and teaching are part of "the work" they do every day. Everyone becomes a lifelong learner as well as a lifelong teacher.

You can let this learner-teacher relationship build informally among team members as they collaborate on projects and define their roles and contributions, or you can take a more formal approach during staff meetings, to leverage particular strengths.

For example, ask members to share three to five things they want to learn and to teach over the next three months; then support every opportunity for two-way mentoring and coaching. Match the employee who's a customer service expert with a new hire who needs those skills fast. How can the expert shorten the learning curve? Does the new hire have anything of value to offer in return? Keep in mind that younger employees—or anyone coming from a different company or industry—may be able to offer the team new insights and ways of doing things.

As a Gen X finance supervisor in public education said of her generation, "We have a willingness to learn, but also have a desire to teach." That desire is also found in many Schwarzkopfers and Boomers who are ready to become master trainers. Uncover that desire and talent in experienced pros of all ages and offer them training in teaching and facilitation skills so they hit the ground running.

Best Practice 7: Banish Job Descriptions

If you really want to energize your team and light their fires, put aside job descriptions—at least for a staff meeting or two—and redefine everyone's tasks and responsibilities. Now that members know the team's mission and goals, as well as all the work that must be done, ask them to divvy up assignments based on each one's talents and preferences.

Facilitate a discussion based on these three questions:

- What work would you love to spend more time doing? Less time doing?

- Which of your talents are presently untapped and would benefit the team?

- Which tasks and responsibilities that you're currently not accountable for would maximize your strengths?

Author and management consultant Theodore Zeldin claims that most people only use 20 to 25 percent of their potential in their present jobs. Maximize that potential by giving team members first dibs on doing the work they love to do. Then, divide up the necessary but less glamorous tasks.

The evidence is clear: When people spend most of their time doing the work they love to do, great performance skyrockets. This process will also give everyone the chance to reevaluate "the work": What routine tasks can be automated, streamlined, or outsourced so people can capitalize on their talents and avoid wasting time on boring or meaningless activities?

Focus your team on their mission, goals, roles, and strengths. Then, let them get on with "the work" that now has direction and meaning.

Three Success Stories

In the course of our workshops, we've met managers who have implemented this best practice and are amazed with the results. For example:

- A nurse manager told us the morale on her floor soared after she allowed the nurses to swap some of their duties. "It astonished me that one hated to do the paper work that another loved. Things as simple as that came to light during our discussion and we made some easy adjustments. They're so much happier now."

- A research manager in a federal agency had an eye-opener when one of her staffers told her she actually loved the challenge of calling very difficult clients. Since everyone else on the team tried to hide from these people, the manager reassigned the hard cases to the expert problem-solver and took some less-challenging duties off her plate.

- A manager of a physical therapy office almost lost an invaluable employee because of a job description. "I knew I couldn't lose her," the manager explained, "but she was already interviewing for another job. So I sat her down and asked her, 'What can I do to keep you?' What it came down to was switching some of the administrative tasks she wasn't good at and didn't enjoy doing. She was marvelous with patients, but not with administrative details. It took some string-pulling, but we redefined her job and I got to keep a very valuable employee."

Best Practices Checklist:
Focus: It's All About the Work

Directions: Below are the seven best practices required to master the skill of focus. Use the checklist to evaluate your effectiveness. Which best practices do you use very well right now? Which do you need to work on right away? What can you do to improve your mastery of this core competency?

Best Practices 1–7	I do this very well	I can improve here
1. Light the fire in the belly	❑	❑
2. Define your team/project mission	❑	❑
3. Clarify the team's work	❑	❑
4. Define each team member's mission	❑	❑
5. Maximize everyone's uniqueness NOW	❑	❑
6. Create learn-teach plans	❑	❑
7. Banish job descriptions	❑	❑
The best practices I need to work on:	How can I master this practice?	

Chapter 7

Communicate Just-in-Time, All the Time

A THIRTYSOMETHING HIT THE BULL'S EYE when she said, "In an increasingly hectic environment, managers are communicating less with their peers and direct reports. This poses a challenge to successfully getting one's job accomplished. I have learned how and when to approach management in hectic situations and communicate effectively to get what I need in a very short period of time."

Why not proactively confront the challenge of effective communication so everyone can work successfully? You can do it by:

- Creating the expectation that even in a hectic environment, communication on all projects, assignments, and important issues will be done just-in-time, all the time

- Helping teams create easy-to-use communication systems that facilitate good communication

We found expert Gen Mix managers across the nation doing just that. Fourteen of their best practices are presented here. We've numbered them as additions to the seven best practices provided in Chapter 6.

Best Practices: Communication

Best Practice 8: Seize Informal Time-Out Times

Anyone who has children knows that the most important family discussions often occur in the car on the way to the grocery store or while you're making dinner, stacking the dishwasher, or tinkering with the lawn mower. Somehow informality facilitates significant sharing.

The same is true in the workplace. Young workers tell us they appreciate informal opportunities to get out of the office to talk with their managers about their work, dreams, capabilities, and outside interests.

A Gen X senior partner in a prestigious financial consultancy told us, "My boss loves going out to lunch, so I make a point of scheduling time to meet with him at his favorite restaurant. He has to eat, so this is my best time with him."

Go for a walk, have coffee, go out to lunch—anything that works for you and your young employees. Be as creative as you can in discovering venues and times that make young people feel comfortable with you. You'll learn more about them during these informal times than in any formal setting.

As for Schwarzkopfers and Boomers, don't buy wholesale the stereotype that they prefer more formal settings even for informal conversations. Test that assumption by asking them their preference. Given the increasing informality in many workplaces, older workers may be as happy as younger ones to capture your undivided attention outside the office.

Best Practice 9:
Establish Formal Time-Outs to Focus on "the Work"

No what matter what generations you're managing, it's imperative to schedule one-on-one, work-related sessions with each team member on a consistent basis. "Consistent" may mean daily or weekly, depending on individual needs. You can't hold people accountable when you don't know what they're doing or how they're progressing, so make these formal meetings a non-negotiable part of your relationship with them.

Create an easy-to-use agenda like the one on the next page to guide these conversations. If both you and your employee come prepared, you can minimize time spent on peripheral conversation and maximize time spent on setting goals, identifying resource needs, and making commitments. Don't be tempted to socialize—do that over coffee or walking to and from the parking lot. If you keep the meetings work focused, they'll be more productive and less apt to tax your time schedule. Once you and you staffers get into the habit of meeting regularly, you'll only need 15 minutes on average to cover the agenda.

Conclude each meeting by documenting the promises and commitments you and your team member have made to each other. Both parties should do this to avoid any confusion or misunderstanding. To facilitate documentation, we recommend you keep a "manager's notebook" and each member keep an "employee's notebook," tracking the results of these meetings. Adopt a simple format. In fact, consider using the agenda form as a template for your tracking system. It's imperative that every meeting end with both parties literally on the same page. By comparing notes, you can see if that is true. No matter what age

—Agenda—
Manager/Team Member Meeting

Manager: _____   Team Member: _____

Date: _____

Work in progress:

My evaluation/feedback:

What I need you to do next:
    Goals   Deadlines   Guidelines

What you need from me:

Commitments:

Signed:

_____   _____
        Manager   Team Member

group you're dealing with, clear communication is challenging; therefore, make each team member a partner in ensuring clarity.

Three Success Stories

During our workshops, we've met managers who claim these formal time-out meetings have revolutionized their relationships with team members. For example:

- A senior manager in a credit union told us that she's cut her staff meeting times by a third because she's dealing with individual issues and problems on a one-to-one basis. Her team is thrilled not to be wasting time on topics that have nothing to do with them.

- An HR director in manufacturing had similar results. She conducts the majority of her one-on-one meetings on the phone because many of her direct reports are in remote locations. Disciplining herself to hold these conversations every week has eliminated most of the conflict she used to experience during formal staff meetings. "We get so much more accomplished when we are together," she said, "and there's so much less stress during our meetings. It's been worth the time and effort."

- Another manager in financial services reported that her direct reports were initially skeptical when she began holding individual meetings. "They thought they were being called to the principal's office," she admitted, "because I only used to meet with them when something was wrong. Now they're so excited about our meeting time that they can't wait to tell me all they've accomplished during the past week. We get so much done in a short period of time. It's been a very positive experience for all of us."

Best Practice 10:
Begin Retention Planning on Day One of Employment

Don't wait for an exit interview to find out why someone is leaving your organization. Instead, make retention planning an essential topic of communication with each staffer from day one of employment. As part of your orientation program, talk one-on-one with new hires about their career planning, the various roles they might play over time in your organization, and what you might have to offer them at each stage of their career. Build this topic into your time-out meetings at least quarterly so you can address these issues in a timely way.

For your current staffers, introduce retention planning during your next time-out meeting and let them know you're doing everything you can to facilitate their career development. Given the free agency attitude of the most talented people of all ages, this conversation can help you avoid getting blind-sided by the valuable staffer who suddenly knocks on your door one day to say farewell because he or she couldn't see any new options or opportunities in your organization.

Best Practice 11:
Circulate Everyone's To-Do Lists and Accomplishments

Ask team members to make to-do lists outlining their team commitments, and to email them to everyone working on a specific assignment or project. This can be done on a daily or weekly basis. The message is "This is what I'm working on today/this week. These are the deadlines and results to which I'm committing."

The practice of making to-do lists is helpful to people who have problems managing their time and staying on track with larger tasks, by requiring them to break down those tasks into smaller, more manageable pieces. And, as the popularity of "mastermind" groups has confirmed, people in general are more productive when they make their commitments public. Procrastination becomes more difficult when "saving face" in front of peers is a motivator.

As a follow-up, ask your staffers to send out brief weekly reports that let others know "This is what I accomplished this week." Such reports not only keep everyone apprised of the work in progress, but also tend to increase motivation. Personal success breeds more success; individual accomplishments inspire and energize others.

Best Practice 12:
Re-think Email as Your Communication Tool of Choice

Researchers claim that email usage expands by 30 percent each year and that 60 percent of what fills business in-boxes is spam. No wonder there's a backlash against the "killer app" that has become a frustrating time-waster.

Some managers have already established EFFs—"Email-Free Fridays"—to encourage real-time, face-to-face conversations. Others are discussing guidelines with their teams to address the email barrage. Questions that you may find worth raising with your team include:

- When is email the appropriate communication vehicle of choice? When is it not?

- What are the guidelines for composing emails and editing their content for clarity?

— Case in point: One thirtysomething financial executive told us he receives 300 emails a day, mostly from Xers and Yers. Many are poorly written, based on mere opinion, composed without thought, and good for nothing but deleting—and wasting the frustrated executive's time.

- What are acceptable turnaround times for email?

- When are phone contacts (not merely voice messaging), face-to-face conversations, or instant messaging (IM) better choices?

- What about de-emphasizing email by using other software tools? For example:

  — Private workplace wikis, which allow people working on the same project to comment on and edit each other's work in real time

  — Microsoft's SharePoint, which helps teams create their own websites to facilitate meetings, manage projects, and create documents without the help of the IT department

  — RSS technology that reduces communication overload by delivering only the information relevant to individuals

Given the popularity of IM among Gen Xers and Yers and blogs among all age groups, email may simply go the way of the typewriter. It just takes too long to attach, archive, track, merge, edit, and respond to documents that could be observed, commented on, revised, and agreed upon in real time.

Best Practice 13: Encourage Members to Ask for Help

Make sure members know that whenever they, as individuals, find themselves stuck, off track, or out of focus, they should immediately ask for help. While some older workers who grew up with "sink or swim" managers may still regard asking for help as a show of weakness, it is the most intelligent approach to getting things done today. You'll find that Gen Yers ask for help instinctively. They may want to appear independent—and are to a great degree—but they also want to know who's available to support them.

Consider using the "Asking for What I Need" form on the following page as a template for strategizing requests. The requests can be verbalized face to face or submitted in written form if people lack immediate access to you or to one another. The requester has the responsibility to suggest how others can deliver on the request. That might mean anything from providing a training opportunity or holding an impromptu team meeting to granting more results-delivery time or doing more in-depth research on a topic. The requester also has the responsibility to indicate deadlines and who will conduct follow-up.

The recipient has the option to deliver the request as stated or to make appropriate revisions.

In our workshops, we've facilitated discussions in which one department or workshift makes requests of another. Groups frequently discover they haven't been clearly communicating their needs or clearly understanding the needs of others. Often people have no idea how some of their activities are adversely affecting their colleagues. Once the air is cleared, everyone can strategize about creating a better working relationship. On either an

—Form—
"Asking for What I Need"

Date:_____

To: _____

From: _____

Subject: I need your help!

Request: _____

_____

_____

Suggestions for delivering the request: _____

_____

_____

Expected date for accomplishment:_____

Follow-up conducted by: _____   Date: _____

Response to request:
- ❏ Accepted as requested.
- ❏ Needs some revision. Let's talk.
- ❏ Hold until this date _____ because:

  _____

- ❏ I can't do this now because: _____

  _____

---

individual or a group basis, encouraging your team members to identify and ask for what they need just-in-time is a winning communication strategy.

Best Practice 14: Create an Experts Database

Facilitate your team's just-in-time access to "the best in the business" by creating an experts database. Include names, contact information, areas of expertise, and experience (including projects successfully completed, innovations introduced or implemented, and customers served). In addition to acting as a valuable networking resource, this database advertises the accomplishments of the key contributors in your organization.

Best Practice 15: Create a Shared-Notes System

If your organization takes a team approach to dealing with customers or clients, it's imperative to have a communication system that records "interaction history."

For example, three Gen Y managers of a new East Coast tanning salon keep detailed computerized notes on their clients' likes and dislikes, scheduling preferences, family interests, birthdays, anniversaries, and favorite tanning specialists. If a client requests a specialist who has the day off, the receptionist is able to personalize a response; for instance, "Jane is sorry she missed you. She asked me to tell you that she hopes your son is feeling better [or that the school play was fun, your car got fixed, and so forth]. She made sure that we will take good care of you today."

According to these young managers, although the salon is surrounded by long-established competition, this personalized approach has quickly won them a loyal customer-base. Given their simple but comprehensive note-sharing system, that level of service is easy to deliver.

We at RainmakerThinking deal with hundreds of organizations, meeting planners, association directors, reporters, and speakers' bureaus every year. Several of us have a hand in delivering our products and services, and each keeps documentation on the salient points of communication with customers, including telephone conversations, email, and snail mail. This information is consistently shared with appropriate team members so everyone is up to speed. Consequently, any member can step in at a moment's notice, fully prepared to continue business without customers having to repeat information or explain previous agreements. Staffers feel prepared and professional; customers are impressed with the just-in-time service they receive.

Best Practice 16:
Hit the Ground Running with Action-Packed Meetings

According to a recent study commissioned by MCI, more than 11 million business meetings are held every day, most of them colossal wastes of time. Everyone knows that, but few are courageous enough to stop the waste. For example, managers in one large governmental agency spend up to 80 percent of their time in meetings. They all agree that most sessions are merely ego shows and power plays, yet no one dares to eliminate them.

Get out of the meeting trap with these guidelines:

* Don't meet just for the sake of meeting—meet only when you have a compelling reason to pull people away from their work and can justify the cost of their hourly

rate. The MCI study reported that employees attend an average of 61.8 meetings a month; if most meetings last two hours—probably a conservative estimate—that's 123.6 working hours. Add to that the 91 percent of surveyed employees who admitted to daydreaming during meetings and the 39 percent who confessed to dozing off, and you have a huge, unjustified expense of time and money. If the only reason for meeting is to convey information that can be delivered via email, reports, or memos, you are squandering valuable time—and wasting money.

- If you must meet, ensure that the meeting's purpose is clear to everyone by defining that purpose in your pre-meeting announcement and again at the start of the session itself.

- Save time during meetings by assigning "homework" beforehand. What do people need to read, think about, bring with them, or come prepared to discuss so the meeting will be more productive?

- Determine beforehand who *really* needs to attend a particular session. Invite everyone on the team, but when it's not a command performance, let those who don't have to be there off the hook. The message is "Feel free to come to this meeting if you are interested and want to offer your input. However, if you are engaged in more pressing work, feel free to pass."

- Keep meetings focused on appropriate issues. Remember, many problems that eat up valuable staff meeting time are individual performance or behavior issues that should be addressed during your regular one-on-one conversations. Be vigilant not to allow these

topics to take over team time. You can be firm and
directive by saying something like, "That's something
I need to talk with so-and-so about. I'll handle it. It's
inappropriate for this meeting, so let's move on."

- Most meetings end in too much talk and too little action
  because of confusion between what was discussed and
  what was decided upon. The remedy? Give everyone a
  discussion/decision form (see the template on the next
  page) to fill out as the meeting progresses.

  Each person will walk away with a clear picture of
  what was left at the discussion level and what actions,
  accountabilities, and deadlines were agreed upon. No
  one will have to wait for meeting minutes. In fact, the
  discussion/decision form can easily substitute for formal
  minutes.

- Give those who want it the chance to learn basic
  facilitation skills; then rotate the leadership of your
  meetings. You can sit back, observe, and offer the
  leader feedback on his or her effectiveness. Remember,
  running a meeting is a key skill for anyone who aspires
  to management.

- Ensure that all your meeting facilitators practice
  "balance of participation." That means they encourage
  everyone to contribute to a topic before the floor is open
  for general discussion. It's important to make sure that
  quieter members who have valuable things to say get
  equal airtime, especially if your team has some
  articulate heavy hitters.

- End each meeting with a quick evaluation. Ask people:
  "On a scale of one to 10, with 10 being the highest, how

Discussion/Decision Form

Issue	Discussion/Decision (Mark decisions w/ asterisks)	Date to Be Effected	Key Person(s) Involved	Review Date	Completion Date

would you rate this meeting? What would it take to make our next meeting a '10'?" Have someone record and distribute the suggestions. Be ready to implement the best ones in time for the next meeting.

Best Practice 17: Evaluate Team Effectiveness

For many people, young or old, becoming a great team player requires learning new skills. Periodically gather together your members to evaluate how well they're working as a team. Ask them to discuss the following questions:

- What are we doing together that's working well?
- What are we doing that's not working well enough?
- What do we need to do to be more effective?
- Who's accountable for the change, and by when?

Decide what training or coaching they need as a team to improve their collaborative efforts.

Best Practice 18:
Evaluate the Effectiveness of Individual Team Members

Determine how well each team member is doing right now in light of your standards for successful team playership. (Feel free to customize standards to make this evaluation even more meaningful to your situation.) Keep the standards in the forefront of everyone's mind by periodically asking members to do a self-evaluation. Use their responses as a topic in your next one-on-one meeting. Recognize successes and set up coaching opportunities for improvement.

The Team Playership Rating Evaluation (see next page) will help you put this best practice into use in your organization.

—Evaluation—
Team Playership Rating

Directions: Using the scale below, rate yourself on the qualities of effective team playership. At our next one-on-one meeting, be prepared to discuss your strengths and one or two areas you want to work on during the next quarter. Bring suggestions for how I can help you improve.

Range of Scale

1 = Ineffective   5 = Moderately effective
10 = Highly effective

The willingness and ability to . . .

1. Work interdependently   1.........5.........10

2. Communicate openly and honestly   1.........5.........10

3. Contribute the best of my talents,
   knowledge, skills, and experience   1.........5.........10

4. Take risks and be innovative   1.........5.........10

5. Focus on problems rather than
   personalities   1.........5.........10

6. See and honor diverse
   perspectives   1.........5.........10

7. Take 100 percent responsibility
   for my roles and goals on the team   1.........5.........10

➡

Evaluation *(concluded)*

8. Behave and speak in ways that move others toward me or at least no further away from me 1..........5..........10

9. Eliminate put-downs, fault-finding, and blaming from my relationships with coworkers 1..........5..........10

10. Build trust, foster collaboration, and support each member's personal development and achievements 1..........5..........10

Suggestions for improvement:

Best Practice 19:
Help Teams Create Conflict-Resolution Guidelines

One of the most difficult skills for teams to learn is how to handle conflicts with one another just-in-time. You can refocus them on their mission, goals, and work, but sometimes personalities will still clash. Since it's counterproductive to have staffers run to you over run-ins with others, help them establish guidelines to get themselves back on track quickly. What principles and guidelines will they follow so conflicts are resolved quickly and respectfully?

A retired Schwarzkopfer from the U.S. Forest Service told us that, late in his career, one of his managers helped his team answer that question; then the agreed-upon guidelines were printed on cards and distributed to everyone. Whenever he had a conflict with someone, he'd pull the card from his wallet and read aloud the guidelines. "It worked," he smiled. "It was pretty hard to continue fighting when we both knew what we had committed to."

A 40-something VP of Media at a prestigious PR firm added that her team members habitually ran to her with their complaints about one another. After asking the obvious question so frequently—"Have you talked this over with so-and-so yet?"—she threw the conflict issue back in their laps. "They know now that their first step is to resolve the issue themselves. The second step is for both of them to come to me. Not one, but both. Interestingly, I'm not a referee much anymore."

Dedicate a team meeting to helping your staffers create their own conflict-resolution guidelines. Make copies of the model "Communication Credo" on the next page and facilitate the exercise that follows it.

Our Team's Communication Credo

❖ We believe in mutual respect, open communication, and the willingness to listen to each other.

❖ We support the principle that we can respectfully agree to disagree and still meet our goals.

❖ We are willing to take responsibility for the quality and depth of our communication.

❖ We have a healthy intolerance for gossip, backbiting, and negativity.

❖ We do not assume to know the intentions behind each other's words or actions until we ask.

❖ We avoid using blame to deflect our responsibility for direct communication.

❖ When we have a disagreement with another team member, we will go immediately to that person to clear the air.

❖ When we communicate together, we will focus on:
  - Issues, situations, and tasks, not on persons
  - Observable behaviors and events
  - The here and the now
  - Specifics rather than generalities

❖ If we cannot resolve a conflict ourselves, we will schedule time to meet with our manager or another appropriate third party to help us work through our issues.

❖ We are willing to forgive one another when our imperfect communication results in misunderstandings and/or hurt feelings.

❖ We will hold one another accountable for the above principles and guidelines.

❖ Exercise: Creating a Communication Credo

1. Divide your team members into groups of four to six participants. For each group, ask someone to volunteer to lead the discussion and someone else to take notes. These notes will ultimately be submitted to a designated person who will print and publish the team's consensus and commitment.

2. Ask each group to read these guidelines carefully and then discuss the following:
   - Which principles can we commit to?
   - Which do we need to revise?
   - Are there others that would be appropriate to our team?
   - What would it mean if we really implemented them?

   Allow 20 to 25 minutes for this discussion.

3. Ask the note takers to make revisions and additions and team members to commit to follow their guidelines.

4. Bring the groups back together and debrief their findings.
   - Where do they agree?
   - Where do they disagree?
   - What revisions and/or additions are still needed?
   - Can every team member make a commitment to follow these guidelines?

5. Designate someone to collate the final results; then determine how and where the results will be displayed. Some groups we've worked with have printed their team credos on card stock and carry them in their wallets or purses. Others have made posters and displayed them in break rooms or employee lounges. Still others have added another level of respect for this process by asking all team members to sign a copy of the credo and then displaying it where everyone can see it.

Whatever method you choose, make sure these guidelines are easily accessible and are used when communication glitches and conflict arise.

Best Practice 20:
Call an Innovation Summit Quarterly or Biannually

This is an enjoyable, high-energy, high-visibility event that sparks creativity and entrepreneurial spirit. The purpose is to focus on one pressing issue (e.g., staffing, scheduling, benefits) or one area of the organization (e.g., marketing, operations, IT, HR) that needs immediate attention.

Participants must be prepared and willing to do the following:

- Toot their own or their team's horn about something they recently implemented that made a difference to the organization. (Starting your summit by focusing on innovations sets the tone for the entire event.)

- Share ideas and seek solutions rather than focus on problems.

These constitute your "ground rules."

Innovation Summit: The Process

1. Begin your summit by clearly defining the issue or area on your agenda. Common sense dictates that clearly understanding a problem leads to clearer solutions. Therefore, ask participants to offer their perceptions and agree on the real obstacles to be hurdled.

2. Set up solutions teams with facilitators, note takers, and reporters. Decide beforehand the best way to configure teams to maximize the creative flow of ideas; for example, form teams from a mix of generations, departments, or disciplines. Ask members not

only to suggest innovative ways to resolve problems but also to prioritize their suggestions, defining deadlines, parameters, and implementers.

3. Instruct note takers to record all the suggestions generated by their teams. After the summit, these should be emailed to a designated staffer, who will synthesize and distribute them immediately so no one's ideas are lost. The fact is, what may not work today may be exactly the innovation you need tomorrow.

4. Return to the large-group format and ask reporters to present their team's priorities. After everyone hears the solutions, ask participants to prioritize those they are ready and willing to implement immediately. What other ideas and strategies must be added to the plan? What are the deadlines and parameters? Who are the parties accountable for implementation?

5. Publicize the solutions and the actions that will be implemented along with idea-owners, implementers, and deadlines. Offer incentives to those individuals and/or teams who successfully implement the best time-, money-, and energy-saving solutions.

The most effective innovations in every organization often come from the "trenches"—from the people of all ages who face a problem or frustration every day. Innovation summits, then, are another opportunity to facilitate communication among your people, empowering them to clear away the obstacles that have an adverse impact on their work.

Best Practice 21: Create an Environment that Encourages Courtesy, Kindness, and Respect

A fortysomething told us: "I had a boss for over a year who never said 'Good morning,' 'Good night,' or 'How was your weekend?' He basically ignored me. We never had staff meetings or one-on-one meetings. He never gave me any unsolicited feedback on my work. This manager did hire me, not inherit me."

Ouch! Such behavior isn't just discourteous; it's downright disrespectful. Contrast that experience to one of another fortysomething, who described her manager this way: "She was 10 years older than I, and she was very friendly with everybody. Very conscious of her well-being, she was also conscious of others . . . She worked with us as adults, not condescendingly. I felt I wouldn't be cast aside if I made a mistake . . . We shared the same huge office, so I could hear her phone conversations. She was as respectful with her boss as she was with her friends and family. She could disagree, and she did; but her respect for human beings was a strong value, and it showed everywhere."

Now that's more like it. Every member of every generation wants to be respected; everyone, regardless of age, deserves courteous treatment. How do courtesy, kindness, and respect permeate *your* team's just-in-time communication?

We went to people-performance expert Shawna Schuh to find out how these behaviors play out in a multigenerational workplace. Shawna explained that today "the rule is to break all the rules. The only challenge is that many people don't even know the rules. Or maybe one generation knows them and another generation doesn't. That can lead to upsetting miscommunication."

She added: "The only way this challenge can be overcome is to go back to a few basics that aren't so much about strict etiquette rules, but more about good old-fashioned kindness. This will keep the courtesy going and generational mixes more productive and profitable."

How can people of all ages show courtesy, kindness, and respect to one another? Shawna recommends eight winning practices:

1. Call people by their formal name when meeting them for the first time, unless you are introduced to them by their first name. It's always a safe bet to err on the side of formality and wait until they invite informality.

2. Introduce all individuals—no matter who they are— whenever they join your business or social circle. This graciousness shows people you value them.

3. Be the first to offer a handshake. This small act of courtesy breaks invisible barriers, makes important connections, and conveys "Welcome! I'm open to engage in conversation with you!"

4. Say "please" and "thank you." These often-forgotten words of courtesy are vital to showing respect and appreciation.

5. Ask others if you can get them something while you're up or while you're out: a cup of coffee, a lunch order, office supplies, whatever. This act of kindness assures people you are thinking of them as well as yourself.

6. Pick up after yourself so others don't have to. This is a kindness no one will notice until you don't do it. Then it will not only be noticed, but also be talked about and resented.

7. Keep gossip or hurtful information to yourself. This is one of the most beneficial best practices for everyone. Gossip is not kind.

8. Ask before you take someone's time. No matter how important you feel your information is, no matter how much you know it will help the other person, *ask* before launching into it. This extends kindness to others, shows respect for their time, and demonstrates that you're etiquette-savvy.

A fortysomething made this plea for courtesy: "I'd like to see people of all generations be more polite and more aware of others . . . Anyone can say 'please,' 'thank you,' or 'pardon me' and be considered courteous. Such behavior reduces the contentiousness of everyday life and allows us to operate effectively."

Mutual respect is exhibited through thoughtful, kind, and courteous behaviors. Model, teach, and expect these behaviors from everyone, regardless of age. They will maximize the positive impact of your team's just-in-time communication.

Best Practices Checklist:
Communicate Just-in-Time, All the Time

Directions: Below are the best practices required to master the skill of just-in-time communication. Use the checklist to evaluate your effectiveness. Which best practices do you use very well right now? Which do you need to work on right away? What can you do to improve your mastery of this core competency?

Best Practices 8–21	I do this very well	I can improve here
8. Seize informal time-out times	❑	❑
9. Establish formal time-outs to focus on "the work"	❑	❑
10. Begin retention planning on day one of employment	❑	❑
11. Circulate everyone's to-do lists and accomplishments	❑	❑
12. Re-think email as your communication tool of choice	❑	❑
13. Encourage members to ask for help	❑	❑
14. Create an experts database	❑	❑
15. Create a shared-notes system	❑	❑
		➡

Best Practices Checklist
Communicate Just-in-Time, All the Time
(concluded)

Best Practices 8–21	I do this very well	I can improve here
16. Hit the ground running with action-packed meetings	❏	❏
17. Evaluate team effectiveness	❏	❏
18. Evaluate the effectiveness of individual team members	❏	❏
19. Help teams create conflict-resolution guidelines	❏	❏
20. Call an innovation summit quarterly or biannually	❏	❏
21. Create an environment that encourages courtesy, kindness, and respect	❏	❏
The best practices I need to work on:	How can I master this practice?	

Chapter 8

Customize! Customize! Customize!

AN EIGHTYSOMETHING MASTER BUTCHER negotiates a 15-hour work week with a neighborhood meat market. He teaches his specialized skills to young non-English-speaking workers. "We use our own sign language," he laughs. "It works fine."

A retired Schwarzkopfer from the heavy-equipment industry returns from a three-week project in Australia. His former employer had lured him back after six years of retirement. They knew his expertise in setting up financial systems far surpassed that of their present employees.

A retired Boomer fire chief who owns a management-training business posts his resume online. Within 10 minutes he receives a call from a fire-equipment distributor looking for a regional sales manager. He negotiates a telecommuting work arrangement, a signing bonus of a month's salary, flexible vacation time, and the chance to promote his training business throughout the company's sales territory.

Welcome to the free market of multigenerational talent. Skilled and talented people of all ages will always be up for grabs—and they know it. They're looking for options and opportunities for learning, growing, adding value, and receiving recognition. If they can find those within your organization, great. You have a strategic advantage over your competitors. If not, they'll go elsewhere, taking your training and their expertise along with them.

As we said earlier, the traditional value of loyalty to an organization, espoused by Schwarzkopfers and Wood-stockers, has been transformed by younger generations into loyalty to one's career and life. And that brand of loyalty has become a top priority for talent of all ages.

Even when people insist they are loyal to their employers, their actions often belie their words.

One day we were talking to a Gen Xer who had just left a financial consulting firm to join its competitor across town. When we mentioned that we do ongoing research on his generation, he snapped, "Oh, I'm not one of those Xers. I believe in commitment, hard work, loyalty—"

We interrupted: "But you just told us you job-hopped."

"Of course," he replied brusquely. "I got a better deal."

*"I'll be loyal to an employer **until** I get a better deal."* That's the new paradigm. We call it "just-in-time loyalty." And it's espoused by workers of all ages riding the free agency wave.

Customize Everything You Can

The best strategy to win the just-in-time loyalty of the best talent in every generation is to customize every aspect of the employer-employee relationship, from scheduling, assignments, and locations to incentives, training, and advancement. "One-size-fits-all" belongs to the workplace of the past; customization is the driving motivator in the present.

Obviously, people have needs that differ not only from one stage of life to another, but from one life challenge to another. For example, childcare is no longer a one-generation issue. With Young Boomers having late-life children and Xers starting families later in their careers, what was once viewed as a young worker's concern has gone intergenerational. Likewise, eldercare was once considered an older worker's issue. Now Gen Xers are being called upon to care for older parents or grandparents.

Whether it's the challenge of the "mommy track" or "daughter track"—or, in some cases, the "daddy" or "son" tracks—the workplace must respond not to the "entitlement" of a generation, but to the needs of individuals.

In addition to different life-stages and challenges, each person on your team holds a different "equity position" in terms of their commitment of time, talent, contribution, enthusiasm, innovation, knowledge, skills, and results. Your goal, then, is to treat them not equally, but equitably. That means people who contribute more, get more; people who contribute less, get less. The most unfair situation is to give everyone the same bonuses, the same salary increases, the same pizza parties when everyone is not working equally hard.

To be perceived as a genuinely fair multigenerational manager, then, you must work very hard at driving high performance and retaining the just-in-time loyalty of your multigenerational talent, one person at a time, one day at a time. To do that, start by embracing the fact that today customization is the key to motivation.

This chapter provides you with four best practices for effectively customizing everything you can in the workplace bargain. Once again, we have numbered these practices as additions to those presented earlier.

Best Practices: Customization

Best Practice 22:
Build a Big Stack of "Bargaining Chips"

Many organizations suffer from the proverbial problem of the left hand not knowing what the right hand is doing. At managers' meetings, we often hear things like "I didn't know we had that benefit. I didn't know we could do that!" One manager almost lost a valued staffer because he was unaware of his company's new maternity-leave benefits until he heard about them from another department.

On the next page, you'll find a brainstorming exercise we use during our Generation Mix workshops that can help you uncover the plethora of incentives and rewards available throughout your organization. Take the initiative to facilitate this activity during a managers' meeting.

As a Gen Mix manager, you must know how much flexibility you have to customize work arrangements and how high your stack of bargaining chips is. For this reason, it's imperative to talk with other managers. What are they doing? What have they tried to do? Which ones are pushing the envelope of their authority to create customized

❖ Brainstorming Exercise: Incentives and Rewards

1. Break your group into teams of four to six members. For each team, ask for a volunteer to lead the exercise and another to take notes on a flipchart. Allow about 15 minutes for the brainstorming session and another 15 to 20 minutes to discuss and clarify the results.

2. Ask the teams to address these two major issues and to brainstorm these questions:

   - Customizing:

     — What customized work arrangements have we negotiated during our work lives that motivated us to stay in a position or an organization?

     — What customized work arrangements have we already negotiated with high-performing individuals to keep them motivated?

     — How can we become even more flexible with customizing great deals for great workers?

   - Bargaining chips:

     — What are all the financial and non-financial bargaining chips at our disposal right now to drive high performance?

     — Are any chips hidden in the system that allies in HR or senior management can help us uncover?

3. After the brainstorming session, open the floor for a free-for-all discussion of what works and what doesn't work; what's negotiable and what's non-negotiable.

arrangements? Who are their allies? Which ones have found allies in HR or senior management? What financial and non-financial bargaining chips have they successfully used to reward their top performers?

Once you've done this, ask yourself: What innovations am I willing to try today? Tomorrow? Next week? Where will I find allies to support me? How will I become a genuinely fair manager who customizes everything I can to drive and reward my high performers, no matter what their age?

The Five Most Sought-After Non-Financial Incentives

If you're strapped for financial incentives, don't underestimate the value of the non-financial. Consider today's five most sought-after non-financials, shown below. Ask yourself: Which ones are age-specific? Which are individual-specific? How can I customize these to meet the needs of my high producers?

1. **Training in marketable skills.** Remember, not only Xers and Yers seek this incentive. Boomers who have been downsized know how precarious the workplace bargain is today. They've learned that amassing marketable skills on their current job may be the key to seizing a better opportunity in the future. And don't forget star Schwarzkopfers and their willingness to learn new things that they perceive as solid contributions.

2. **Control over schedules.** For all ages, flexible scheduling remains one of the most desirable work arrangements. Whether a staffer is a Gen X mother with a new baby, a Gen Y teacher who wants to travel in the summer, or a Schwarzkopfer or Woodstocker nearing retirement, "stretch" is key. Organizations that want to attract and

➡

The Five Most Sought-After Non-Financial Incentives
(concluded)

retain talent must become more creative at providing
flexible schedules. (See our discussion of flexibility later
in this chapter.)

3. **Control over assignments.** Whether you offer an ace
Gen X roofer the choice of the next work site, or an outstanding Gen Y government analyst the opportunity to
make a presentation on Capitol Hill, or a seasoned
Boomer salesperson the chance to train a team of
new hires, giving high performers control over their
assignments is a winning strategy.

4. **Control over location.** This may mean going to another
country, state, city section, or workplace floor. Or, it may
simply mean decorating a cubicle to add a touch of
creativity to a workspace.

5. **Choice of coworkers.** In the best of all possible worlds,
people would "just get along." In the real world, sometimes
even the best efforts to resolve personality conflicts, or to
reconcile different work styles, simply fail. The fact is,
some people work better with one worker than another,
and will lose motivation otherwise. Allowing discretion in
the choice of coworkers thus may serve as a reward for
high performers.

Think of these non-financials as internal escape hatches,
giving people the chance to reinvent themselves right within
your company. Letting high producers of all ages move into
new skill areas, work with new people, take on new tasks
and responsibilities, work different hours, or work from a new
location is a Gen Mix management imperative—and one that
pays off handsomely in morale, motivation, and productivity.

Best Practice 23:
Let Everyone Know What's on the Table

Once you recognize the authority you have to customize deals and to reward people with financial and non-financial bargaining chips, the next step is to communicate to your team members that high performance is non-negotiable. Everyone, no matter what their seniority or age, is expected to do their best work every single day. And you are going hold them accountable and track their results so you can reward them based on one criterion only: performance.

Level the playing field for incentives by focusing on individual team members and taking the following approach:

1. Ensure that members each know exactly what's expected of them to keep their jobs, salary, and benefits. That's the baseline.

2. Let members know how and when you'll expect them to meet more ambitious goals and, consequently, earn a more flexible schedule, a spot bonus, a choice assignment—whatever it is that engages them. Then work hard to keep this process transparent. As you negotiate equitably with each individual, you'll eliminate the myriad of conflicts that arise over the issue of fairness.

3. Find out what's important to each member, either through formal conversations or informal observation. What lights their fire, what keeps them focused and energized? Periodically put this topic on the agenda

of your regular one-to-one conversations, since a person's needs and expectations can change even in a matter of months.

You also may want to balance this individual approach with a team approach. To do so, engage your team in a brainstorming session about the financial and non-financial rewards meaningful to them. With their list at hand, you can let them know up front what's available, what's off the charts, and what you will negotiate about with HR.

Above all, your multigenerational team members need to know that you're committed to holding all of them accountable for high performance and that you will bend over backwards to keep their morale and motivation soaring through customized recognition and rewards.

Best Practice 24:
Offer Incentives That Have "Three-F Appeal"

During our work with various industries, we have found that incentives and rewards based on the three F's—family, fun, and flexibility—are among the most popular of bargaining chips. How creative are you in each of these areas?

❖ Family Appeal

- A managing director at TLP, a Dallas-based marketing agency, told us about his company's family advocacy program, TLParents. He explained that the program "sponsors in-house parties for kids and arranges time off for parents to attend parent-teacher conferences or take their youngsters to doctors' appointments. Overall, the program

---

A Case Study in Customization

Let's eavesdrop on a multigenerational conversation that could take place on any Friday afternoon in any organization in any part of the country.

"Wait a minute, Cynthia. Where are you going?" a Boomer says, looking up from his desk. "You're not leaving, are you? It's only three. We don't close until five-thirty."

"My kids have soccer games on Fridays, John, and I want to be there," the Gen X new staffer responds. "This was the arrangement I asked for when I signed on, and this is what Jeff agreed to. Before I accepted this job, I negotiated for what I need."

"That's not fair," chimes in a Schwarzkopfer. "I've been here for 23 years and I can't just up and leave."

"What's not fair," a new Gen Y employee complains, "is treating everyone the same when we all produce results at a different pace. If I can reach my goals in four days and it takes you five, why should I have to put in more time? I should have Fridays off!"

Imagine you are Jeff, their Gen X manager. How will you clear the air with your team on Monday morning and get them back on track, working collaboratively?

---

makes sure that being an employee [at TLP] doesn't exclude being a parent too."

- Childcare was a top priority for the 120 young staffers at a small ad agency in southern California. After listening to their needs, the agency discovered that the staffers were willing to contribute $150 a week per family for onsite childcare. Consequently, it hired one teacher for every four youngsters, and provided playpens in offices so parents could spend lunchtime with their children. The result? High morale and high productivity and retention rates.

- Boomers with grown children don't need childcare, but many of them do need eldercare. Whether you offer older workers information about eldercare facilities or estate planning or give them flexibility to take parents to doctors' appointments and to do their weekly shopping, find innovative ways to address an issue that will become even more critical for Boomers—and Xers—during the next decade.

- Many organizations ensure that families consistently know how much they appreciate members. Some send letters of appreciation, flowers, or restaurant gift certificates to employees' homes to thank supportive families. One even rewarded a spouse with a gift certificate to a luxurious spa. Why? Because her husband had just returned from three productive weeks on the road and the company wanted to recognize her for taking on all the family duties while he was away.

- Businesses from credit unions to bookstores offer laundry pick-up services for their employees so there's one less chore for them to do at home. One elementary school even installed a washer and dryer onsite as an incentive for parent volunteers.

- After hiring a Gen Y college grad for her large Midwestern bank, an HR director sent a letter home to the grad's parents, expressing her delight at having him on board and complimenting him on his interviewing skills. She invited the parents to visit the bank to see the environment in which he would be working and to meet his manager and coworkers.

• Savvy managers are addressing the "family-friendly backlash" among workers who don't have family connections right now. Such workers complain they're the ones picking up the slack when parents go to those PTA meetings or doctors' appointments. Don't let this deter you from using family-focused incentives, but do recognize it as another wake-up call for customization. What can you offer single workers that will be as valuable to them as the rewards above are to family members?

❖ Fun Appeal

• This is an area where you can let your imagination stretch as far as your budget will allow. There's virtually no limit to what organizations will do to energize their teams with fun—and usually low-cost—activities.

• Everyone loves food and the socializing that comes with it. Some organizations offer "Bagel Wednesdays," "Popcorn Thursdays," or "Ice Cream Social Fridays" as ongoing events.

Others sponsor ethnic-food potlucks as a way to celebrate diversity as well as bring people together. One company even published a diversity cookbook with easy-to-use recipes and educational pieces about their origins.

- Throw "wind downs": one-time events to celebrate the end of a project or stressful stretch of time. These might include onsite parties, trips to sporting events or amusement parks, or team lunches at a favorite restaurant.

- Maximize the talent within your talent. For example, one Boomer manager explained to us what she did when a staffer showed talent in an area outside her job description: "I allowed this talent to bloom, and we were both rewarded with a sense of growth. Mine was noticing an emerging talent and hers was noticing a talent she did not know she had. I will never forget the sense that something bigger was happening here."

"Something bigger" can happen when you realize that the people working with you every day are not only engineers, designers, nurses, accountants, salespeople, or telemarketers, but also poets, painters, photographers, dancers, musicians, songwriters, storytellers, athletes, landscapers, and fine-cuisine chefs. They have all kinds of talents that could add richness to your environment.

Finding that talent and letting it shine within the world of work gives people of all ages a chance to see others in a completely new light. Take the manager who was about to hire a professional photographer to illustrate a new brochure. In the course of an informal chat, he discovered that one of his staffers was an amateur photographer. He asked to see the young man's work, and was so impressed with its quality that he hired to him to "moonlight" on the project.

Such talent can be used for charitable purposes, too. For example, some organizations collaborate with groups like the United Way to sponsor fund-raising talent shows that put their own people in the spotlight. We at RainmakerThinking worked with a nonprofit organization that held an annual coffeehouse where people of all ages shared their music, poetry, and visual art.

The fact is, the talent within your talent can generate excitement and enthusiasm that spills over into everyday collaboration and productivity. How can you unleash it so "something bigger" happens on your team?

• Appoint a "fun raiser" and give him or her a catchy title like "The Pharaoh of Fun." (Ben and Jerry's calls theirs "Granter o' Wishes.") Create a fun budget and give your fun raiser the responsibility to get everyone involved in how the budget is used. Since what is "fun" for one person may be drudgery for another, the more choices you offer, the more likely it is that people will find an activity custom-fit for what they enjoy.

❖ Flexibility Appeal

• Remember that time is a valuable commodity. In fact, most people tell us that time is more important to them than money. Whenever we discuss custom-ized deals in our workshops, nine out of ten involve flexible work arrangements. For example, one senior manager at a large East Coast bank told us she had just negotiated coming to work at 11 a.m. on Mondays. Why? She found she could get an early tee time at her golf club more easily on a weekday. Since she worked from home on weekends, her manager readily agreed to the arrangement.

We've heard of many young parents who are so valuable in the workplace that their managers have created work schedules that combine office time with telecommuting. A manager in a multinational told us that one new mother does five days of work in four. She's so motivated to be at home with her child that she's out-producing the typical nine-to-fiver.

One manager in a federal government agency offered a telecommuting "carrot" to a mediocre employee as a challenge to raise his performance. Not only did his productivity soar, but he quickly tested the fairness of the system. As his manager recounted, "One week he blew it. His results were less than average so we pulled his telecommuting arrangement. He had to come into the office every day the next week and re-earn the privilege of working from home. Since we did that, he's remained a top performer. He doesn't want to lose his 'carrot' again!"

The Director of a VA hospital recounted that he gave a $2500 bonus to a staffer who had successfully completed an exceptionally difficult assignment. He was surprised to see her in his office within hours. "I'm going to give this back to you," she said, handing him the check. "I'd like to have a week off in September instead to spend time with my family."

"That $2500 was worth more than two weeks of her salary," the Director explained, "but time off was more valuable to her. I agreed to give it to her."

One of our interviewees added she is even willing to give back nine percent of her salary to work from home. "The nine percent," she told us, "represents approximately how much I spend monthly for gas, meals out due to lack of time to prepare them, and someone to do my family's laundry every week. I believe I can realistically perform my job duties from home."

- Be creative at negotiating time off and flexible scheduling as incentives. Here are four effective approaches we've discovered:

  — Issue "Take-a-Day" certificates redeemable within 90 days. It entitles the bearer to a day off as a reward for producing extraordinary results.

  — Offer summer (or other seasonal) flex hours when business slows down. Some companies offer a choice of five paid Fridays off during the summer; others close their offices at 3 p.m. each Friday. Some organizations completely close down between Christmas and New Year's Day, making it a mandatory vacation time for everyone. Since their clients are too involved in holiday activities to need extensive services, it makes sense to let employees enjoy the holidays without the stress of work.

  — Offer holiday work-volunteer opportunities. In some industries, like health care and retail, working on holidays is imperative. Before you go through the hassle of trying to schedule holidays equitably, why not give team members the opportunity to volunteer to work? The payoff? In addition to time and a half (or whatever monetary bonus you offer), give them an extra paid day (or two!) off for each holiday worked. Since holidays have different value and meaning to different people, you may be pleasantly surprised to discover the trade-offs staffers are willing to make for that kind of incentive.

— Empower your staffers to negotiate work schedules among themselves. Whether dealing with emergency on-call schedules like those in hospitals, shift-change schedules like those in manufacturing, or basic daylong schedules like those in many businesses, savvy managers have set clear guidelines and then let employees work out the details themselves.

Best Practice 25:
Set Up Career Development Accounts

This is a no-brainer. You have to customize training to meet the needs of your age-diverse team. It's true that most people in every generation prefer the hands-on, practical approach to training, where there is a clear relationship between what they're learning, how necessary it is to their jobs, and how soon they'll use it. It's also true that older generations prefer classroom-style training, where they can interact with an instructor and with one another, while many Xers and Yers prefer the self-paced, independent-study style of computer-based training. Online education is great for some workers; it's a turn-off for others.

Along with your training department, you have to decide which modalities fit which individuals and which content is appropriate for which learning vehicle. Here, we're not talking about the training you must give everyone of every age so they can do their jobs very well. Rather, we're talking about a customized incentive called a "career development account" (CDA) that rewards your talent with an innovative learning opportunity.

A Boomer HR professional defined the CDAs in her organization as "budgeted training dollars allocated to individuals to use according to broad guidelines." She explained, "We generally approve expenditures on anything related to self-development because we believe that all development enhances performance in some way."

If classes in yoga or tai chi facilitate relaxation and focus, how appropriate for the workplace! If classes in literature, art, or music expand the imagination and touch the spirit, why not? It will spill over into their creativity at work. Let your staffers of all ages who are interested in such self-improvement opportunities—and remember Boomers "invented" self-improvement—know how they can add dollars to their CDAs through their performance.

Obviously, many of the incentives we described above are attractive to all generations. Some may be more enticing at one life stage; others at another. Whatever the case, your challenge as a Gen Mix manager is to hold people of all ages accountable for high performance and be ready to drive that performance through rewards that are meaningful and personal. This is hard work, no doubt, but it's the kind of work that will raise your team's morale, productivity, and quality of results exponentially.

Best Practices Checklist:
Customize! Customize! Customize!

Directions: Below are the four best practices required to master the skill of customization. Use the checklist to evaluate your effectiveness. Which best practices do you use very well right now? Which do you need to work on right away? What can you do to improve your mastery of this core competency?

Best Practices 22–25	I do this very well	I can improve here
22. Build a big stack of bargaining chips	❏	❏
23. Let everyone know what's on the table	❏	❏
24. Offer incentives that have "Three-F Appeal" • Family Appeal • Fun Appeal • Flexibility Appeal	❏	❏
25. Set up career development accounts	❏	❏
The best practices I need to work on:	**How can I master this practice?**	

PART THREE
From Retirees to Teens:
Four Opportunities
for the Taking

What You Can Expect

AS THE GENERATIONAL SHIFT continues to accelerate during the next decade, organizations will face four urgent multi-generational challenges that require their immediate attention:

1. Retaining the wisdom, knowledge, and expertise of retiring Schwarzkopfers and Woodstockers for as long as possible

2. Overcoming the midlevel leadership crisis by building Gen X and Y bench strength

3. Helping young leaders manage workers old enough to be their parents or grandparents

4. Teaching teens to become customer service experts adept at maintaining customer loyalty

Each chapter in this section focuses on one of these challenges. We'll discuss the trends we see emerging right now, and offer you practical suggestions on how to turn those trends into strategic opportunities. If you seize such opportunities right now, you will lessen the negative impact of the labor and leadership shortages that, experts predict, will occur within the next four years.

Chapter 9

Turning Gray to Gold: How to Mine the Riches in Seasoned Talent

"Employers need to realize that some of us older professionals have grown children. We may be divorced or widowed, and we have incredible skills and the time to work. And we want to work."

—A Woodstocker computer expert

SOME RESEARCHERS PREDICT that by 2010 the United States will face a labor shortage with 10 million more jobs than available workers to fill them. While the real extent of this shortage is still being debated, the fact remains that you and your organization must not only create knowledge transfer programs immediately, but also retain the experience and maturity of your older workers for as long as possible.

We already know, in 2006, that two experienced workers are leaving the workplace for every one inexperienced worker who arrives. Too many organizations haven't "gotten" the ramifications of that imbalance and are merely stumbling through this Generational Shift rather than taking decisive action. On one hand, they report that retaining skilled labor is one of their major priorities; on the other, they fail to recognize that successfully doing so requires addressing the needs of an aging workforce.

Yet, for those organizations who are ready to address those needs, good news is on the horizon. The negative impact of an acute labor shortage may well be lessened by two major emerging and merging sociological trends:

1. Long-held workplace stereotypes about older workers are crumbling.

2. Schwarzkopfers and Boomers are redefining aging and retirement. Many not only need to work, but want to work past the typical retirement age.

Breaking Down the Stereotypes

The workplace has traditionally been a bastion of ageism. As if age and experience were negatives, organizations retired or laid off higher-paid older workers without a second thought. Now they're not only having second thoughts, but third and fourth ones.

First of all, the perception that workers over age 50 cost more than younger workers was recently debunked by Towers Perrin, a global professional services firm. In their report, "The Business Case for Workers Age 50+," they found that the extra compensation and benefits costs for attracting and retaining 50-plus workers runs "from negligible to three percent." And that "negligible to three percent" is quickly erased when organizations factor in savings in training time, building credibility with customers, access to organizational memory, and dozens of others intangibles that engaged, motivated older workers bring to the table every day.

Think about it: When faced with a crisis, which members of your team can you count on? Who are best equipped to help you with as few learning, training, and growing pains as possible? More than likely, your choices are Schwarzkopfers and Boomers.

Second, it's now common knowledge that older workers are less risky and more loyal to their employers than their younger colleagues. According to the US Labor Department, the median tenure of workers 55 to 64 is three and a half times higher than that of workers 25 to 34. These seasoned pros also have lower absentee rates, take fewer sick days, adapt to new technologies successfully, have more experience with "soft" communication skills, and are more physically fit than expected. They also have a strong work ethic that often rubs off on younger workers.

In addition, some of the characteristics employers say they now value in a workforce are in sync with older workers. These characteristics include:

- Commitment to get quality work done right and on time
- Loyalty and dedication to the organization
- A strong customer-service attitude
- The ability to handle crises with a calm maturity
- The ability to get along well with diverse coworkers
- Skill at the basics of reading writing, and math

And the great news for older workers is that they're getting new jobs at an annual rate of 4.1 percent, more than double the .8 percent rate of the general population.

Of course, true to form, Baby Boomers are leading the stereotype-breaking charge. The energetic creators of

---

You Can't Keep a Talented Person Down . . .

After 30 years in the insurance industry, a seventysomething retiree creates his own consulting firm. His expertise translates into books that make him a sought-after speaker at industry conferences.

A physically fit, engaging seventysomething government employee confides, "Don't tell anyone how old I am. I'm never going to retire. I have too much energy and too much to offer."

An eightysomething health-care worker says she's retired three times already and couldn't stand it. "I was bored. I want to contribute."

"youth culture" are redefining what people in their fifties and sixties can and cannot do, want and don't want to do. Echoing Gloria Steinem, Boomers are proclaiming, "This is what 50—or 60—looks like and can accomplish. And just wait until we reach our seventies, eighties, nineties. The good times will keep on rolling!"

Typical of the Boomer propensity to steal the spotlight, *Parade Magazine* teamed up with the Harvard School of Public Health and the MetLife Foundation in December 2005 to sponsor a contest to name a new life-stage between 60 and 80 years of age. Since Woodstockers' life expectancy is now projected to be 83—and millions fully intend to live well into their nineties—they will not tolerate being called "seniors," "elderly," or "old." Some of the creative suggestions include the Sage Age, the XYZ Group (eXtra Years of Zest), and the Age of Dignity. Perhaps, the last social stand for the Me Generation will indeed be a "longevity revolution."

Redefining Retirement

Along with powerhouses in the Schwarzkopf Generation, Boomers are also redefining retirement in ways that will make an impact on future generations. They're set to prove that retirement is not a date on a calendar, but a process— and organizations who can extend that process for as long as it's beneficial to both sides of the desk will have a competitive advantage for the next 10 to 20 years.

According to the AARP, "Seventy percent of workers who have not retired reported that they plan to work into their retirement years or never retire; almost 50 percent expected never to retire." Why? They need the money and health benefits, they want to remain productive and useful, they enjoy interesting work, they want to stay mentally and physically fit, or all of the above. (See AARP Study, "Attitudes of Individuals 50 and Older Toward Phased Retirement," March 2005.)

With those numbers in mind, you have a tremendous opportunity to circumvent the knowledge-experience drain and lessen the impact of a labor shortage in your organization. Here are three strategic imperatives to help you seize that opportunity right now:

1. "Hog-tie" your soon-to-retire talent.
2. Post a "welcome back" sign for all valued retirees.
3. Put out the welcome mat for the 50-plus set.

I. "Hog-tie" Your Soon-to-Retire Talent

Find out from HR who on your team or in your department is slated to retire during the next one to three years. Set up a one-on-one meeting to discuss options with these workers. Ask them the key question: "What would it take for you to stay with us beyond your retirement date?"

You may find there's nothing that would entice some people right now—they may need time off to regroup and re-energize before they realize the grass isn't always greener in the retirement arena. If this happens, make sure these workers maintain their connection to your organization (a useful way to do this is by establishing an alumni association, which is discussed later in this chapter).

For those willing to be enticed, be prepared with a menu of attractive options to offer them. For example, consider the following possibilities:

- Flexible work arrangements. High on the wish lists of older workers, these include flexible schedules, telecommuting, job sharing, new locations, new jobs, and new training opportunities.

- Short-term sabbaticals (two to three months). Give people the initial breather they need as they approach retirement age, and then, upon their return, continue to offer sabbaticals at periodic intervals. Even unpaid respites of a few weeks' duration may be very attractive to some older workers and can reduce burnout while helping to retain them.

- "Phased retirement." A comparatively new concept, phased retirement will become an increasingly important option as the workforce continues to age. This arrangement allows people to leave the workplace gradually by "phasing down" their workload and hours (see sidebar).

Obstacles to Hurdle

While many organizations are open to trying phased retirement, some obstacles still need clearing before this arrangement becomes more attractive to employees as well as employers. For example, you and your human resources department need to discuss what impact phasing down would have on employees' pensions and health-care coverage.

In addition, current regulatory restrictions make it difficult for employers to hire back retired workers into a phased retirement arrangement. The federal government is currently reviewing these restrictions and, hopefully, changes are on the horizon. As retaining older talent in the workforce becomes recognized as beneficial not only to employees but to employers and society at large, age-friendly policies will become the norm.

Remember: As Boomers go, so goes the workplace. And phased retirement may become very attractive to that generation when they're educated about the possibilities, and when pension and benefits penalties are reduced or eliminated.

- Part-time work. Offer people the chance to continue adding value on a part-time basis as flex-timers, floaters, periodic temps, or consultants.

- "Bridge jobs." These allow people to work outside their former positions and continue to leverage their skills while providing an opportunity for new experiences, assignments, and coworkers.

Whatever path you take, one thing is clear: It's vital to make retaining your about-to-retire workforce a strategic imperative. If you position personalized work arrangements as the new status symbol awarded to highly valued older contributors, you will have a stack of powerful bargaining chips with which to negotiate with this invaluable workforce. Then, if you are very flexible in creating "customized deals" on a person-by-person basis, you can gracefully and effectively "hog-tie" these experienced contributors for as long as possible.

2. Post a "Welcome Back" Sign for All Valued Retirees

Five years ago, when we were researching the first edition of this book, some industries were already desperate to re-hire their retired workers as consultants, project leaders, or part-timers. The health-care industry, for example, was facing crisis-level nursing shortages, and had begun exploring ways to recruit retired nurses as part-timers without reducing their retirement benefits.

Immediately after September 11, 2001, the FBI, which has a mandatory retirement age of 57, hired back retirees in droves because more than 40 percent of its worldwide workforce had five or fewer years of experience—and experience was a crucial commodity for a country in crisis.

The same rehiring trend hit education, where teacher shortages were projected to reach crisis proportions within the next five years. Then, by 2004, some state and county governments began to lose thousands of their most experienced workers to the lure of retirement packages slated for dramatic cuts in 2005. Government workers left

---

For Your Information . . .

- Forty states will have a dearth of registered nurses by 2020. Today, it's 30 states.
- Teachers' organizations predict that by 2010 there will be 150 thousand to 200 thousand openings in elementary and secondary schools. Other experts project a shortage of 2.2 million teachers in the next decade.
- In many federal and state government agencies, 50 percent of the employees will be eligible for retirement within the next five years.

---

behind watched their older colleagues walk out the front door one day, only to return through the back door as consultants or part-timers the next.

By now, the "boomerang" employee has become a necessary fixture in some industries and may well be the "ex-factor" that staves off labor shortages in others during the decade to come. Post your "welcome back" sign to valued employees such as this by:

- Creating your own alumni association
- Finding out what's important to working retirees

Creating Your Own Alumni Association

Several years ago, we worked with a company that surveyed departing employees and discovered that 80 percent of them would be willing to return in the future. This was great news, since it spoke of how highly the company was perceived by its workers. However, this data remained just that: data. It wasn't used productively because this organization had no formal or informal methods of discovering under what terms people would be willing to return. It also had no channels of communication to stay in touch with them, keeping them informed about the organization, their coworkers, and opportunities for work. Rather than capitalizing on the huge talent network it had at its disposal, the company spent time, money, and energy advertising and recruiting in conventional ways. You can't afford to make the same mistake today.

According to Cem Sertoglu, founder of SelectMinds, a company that creates Web-based software for employee alumni programs, "It is up to 50 percent cheaper to recruit ex-employees, 40 percent cheaper to get them fully productive, and they tend to stay twice as long as new hires." These statistics make a powerful financial argument for paying close attention to your retirees.

What do you need to do now? Spearhead an initiative to create an alumni newsletter and alumni networking groups—based on those in academia—to keep retirees in touch with you and one another. Update them on what's happening within the organization, with their former coworkers, and with others who have left the organization. Advertise all the opportunities available to them for project work, consulting, and full-time/part-time work arrangements. In other words, turn your newsletter and networking groups into major recruiting tools.

Organizations who have already implemented employee alumni programs, and who now re-recruit talent from their own network, report dramatically slashing their advertising and recruiting budgets. Through these channels of com-munication, they've built reserve armies of experienced professionals who are ready and willing to work—at least

---

Matchmaking Websites

In addition to creating their own alumni networks, some large organizations like Boeing, Shell, General Electric, and Toyota are advertising positions for retirees on "matchmaking" websites such as AlumniInTouch, SelectMinds, YourEncore, and RetiredBrains.com. Not only do they encourage their retirees to sign up for several sites, but they also have access to a larger pool of older talent from a variety of industries at their fingertips.

---

some of the time. And it's a cadre of professionals who already know their business, their customers, their policies and procedures.

Since this strategy works well with retirees, there's another inherent benefit in a talent network: It can expand to include anyone of any age who leaves your organization in good standing. Rather than considering them disloyal job-hoppers, consider the time they spend gathering skills and experience outside your organization as a value-added proposition upon their return. The grass isn't always greener when people leave organizations, and some recognize that sooner or later. Distinguish yourself as a manager and as an organization by letting good employees of all ages know that when they leave, a "welcome back" sign will be waiting for them whenever they want to return. Then, keep in touch, keep in touch, keep in touch.

Finding Out What's Important to Working Retirees

Three years ago, the AARP issued a report called "Staying Ahead of the Curve 2003: The AARP Working in Retirement Study." They wanted to find out which benefits and employer characteristics were most important to working retirees. These were the top "very important" or "somewhat important" responses:

- Working in an environment where employee opinions are valued
- Being able to take time off to care for relatives
- Working for a company that lets its older employees remain employed for as long as they wish to work
- Having new experiences
- Being able to learn new skills
- Being able to set own work hours

None of these responses or "demands" is surprising or revolutionary. They sound just like the multigenerational needs and expectations we've been describing throughout this book.

The worksheet on the next page is based on this study's findings. Use it to evaluate your own organization's readiness to create a retiree-friendly environment. Then poll your current Schwarzkopfers and Woodstockers about which items would be attractive to them. Add their recommendations to your list, and be armed with these bargaining chips when re-recruiting your retirees.

3. Put Out the Welcome Mat for the 50-Plus Set

Many Boomers for whom work and identity are synony-mous may retire from an organization, but they still want to work. What that "work" will look like, however, is currently open for discussion. A new trend is emerging among Boomers that some experts have dubbed "unretirement," "re-careering," or "career shifting." Whatever the term, some

Evaluation Checklist:
Welcome Back

Directions: Specifically, how do you provide what working retirees want in each of the following areas? (Use these as bargaining chips when re-recruiting retirees.) How can you do this better in the future? Make this the focus of positive changes.

Areas	What we offer now	Where we need to improve
1. Working in an environment where employee opinions are valued	❏	❏
2. Being able to take time off to care for relatives	❏	❏
3. Working for a company that lets its older employees remain employed for as long as they wish to work	❏	❏
4. Having new experiences	❏	❏
5. Being able to learn new skills	❏	❏
6. Being able to set own work hours	❏	❏
Further recommendations:		

> "You may well have too much intellectual curiosity and too much enthusiasm for life ever to retire . . . Forget about retirement. Forget about planning for it. Just find something that you love to do."
>
> — Marshall Goldsmith, "Why Even Thinking About Retirement Can Be A Bad Idea," FAST Company, January 2004

of the most highly educated Boomers aren't merely going to job-hop; they're going to career-hop. Sounding like Gen Yers, they're seeking jobs with a greater sense of purpose that will allow them to give something of value back to the community. Understandably, nonprofits are abuzz about the contributions even a small percentage of the huge Boomer population could make to their enterprises either as paid or unpaid volunteers.

Whether you are a for-profit or not-for-profit, one the most significant paradigm shifts you'll need to make is seeing a prospective worker as far more than a former job title. In fact, when beginning to hire career-hopping professionals, you'll have to ignore those job titles and focus purely on skills and experience. These are the transferable commodities that make these Boomers so valuable.

Prepare for this new perspective and put out the welcome mat by:

- Recruiting proactively
- Offering age-specific benefits

Recruiting Proactively

A growing number of organizations are seizing the opportunity to hire highly trained, skilled pros by actively recruiting older workers. In fact, the AARP has begun to identify "Featured Employers" that have "an aggressive program" for employing mature workers. On its list are companies like Home Depot, CVS/Pharmacy, Express Personnel Services, Kelly Services, MetLife Inc., Pitney Bowes, Verizon, and Walgreens.

How is your organization creating a reputation in your region as an age-friendly "Featured Employer"? How are you making older workers part of your organizational "image" in the community?

Offering Age-Specific Benefits

One strategy these companies use to attract the 50-plus crowd is to offer them age-specific benefits. The most attractive include:

- Financial services counseling and workshops
- Health benefits with extra enticements such long-term care insurance and superior dental and vision plans
- Eldercare education and support
- Wellness programs
- Training opportunities
- Mentoring opportunities
- Flexible options such as job sharing, part-time work, flextime, and telecommuting

Use the worksheet on the next page to evaluate the benefits that you and your organization offer right now.

Evaluation Checklist:
Attracting 50-Plus Talent

Directions: Using the checklist below, evaluate the benefits that you and your organization offer now or will be able to offer in the near future.

Benefits	We offer this now	We can offer this in the near future
1. Financial services counseling and workshops	❑	❑
2. Health benefits including: • Long-term care insurance • Dental plan • Vision plan	❑	❑
3. Eldercare education and support	❑	❑
4. Wellness programs	❑	❑
5. Training opportunities	❑	❑
6. Mentoring opportunities	❑	❑
7. Flexible options including: • Job sharing • Part-time work • Flextime • Telecommuting	❑	❑

Which benefits can you offer in the near future to make your workplace even more attractive to older workers?

The Time to Act Is Now

As the workforce continues to age—by 2010 almost one in three workers will be at least 50—and knowledge and experience increasingly become value-added propositions, every organization will be scrambling to create a reputation as an age-friendly workplace. Beat the rush right now by acting on the strategies we've discussed in this chapter:

- Keeping your soon-to-retire employees for as long as possible

- Posting "welcome back" signs, such as alumni groups and preferred enticements, for all valued retirees

- Actively recruiting and hiring talent in the 50-plus crowd

If you take decisive steps in these areas today, you will indeed avoid the knowledge-experience drain, stave off the labor shortage, and stay ahead of the competition for years to come. The urgent question is, do you and your organization have the determination to make the workplace transformations these strategies require?

The graying of the workforce is a given; turning this demographic into a goldmine is your golden opportunity.

Chapter 10

Heading Off the Midlevel Leadership Crisis: Who's Going to Take Charge?

NO MATTER HOW SEVERE the overall skilled-labor shortage may become, there is already an urgent staffing crisis facing most organizations: a gap in midlevel leadership talent and a gap in workers who would typically provide the bench strength for midlevel leadership positions. Why this leadership crisis? Four reasons:

1. Demographics. The "prime-age" workforce—those 35- to 45-year-olds who hold most midlevel manager positions—is shrinking. According to the Bureau of Labor Statistics, by 2011 their numbers will drop by more than 10 percent.

2. Among those in the midlevel manager pool, a smaller percentage than in the past have followed the traditional ladder-climbing path to midlevel leadership roles.

3. A surprising number of people in that midlevel manager pool do not want leadership roles. They want status, prestige, and rewards, but not the responsibility that comes with supervisory and managerial positions.

4. Most organizations have neglected to develop new alternative paths to developing midlevel leaders.

All together this has created a midlevel leadership gap in organizations of all shapes and sizes in just about every industry; and that gap is rapidly widening. That means you and your organization are facing a dual challenge: a labor shortage in general and a dearth of leadership candidates in particular.

How well are organizations responding? Not very. Some tell us they're just beginning to think about succession planning; others claim they'll be introducing leadership development programs within a year; still others are not even aware of the urgency. Yet, every day we meet cutting-edge Boomer managers in these same organizations who know all about the crisis. They're living in the midst of it every day. They wear more "hats" than ever before, and find themselves accountable for more projects, more people, more demands—and with fewer resources and less help to get the work done. Out of desperation, some of them have already started to make leadership development their top priority.

How are they doing that? These savvy managers have begun to scout out the next generation of leaders on their teams and coach them in real-life management skills. They know that classroom training is only valuable to a point, so they find opportunities to help high-potential leadership candidates translate learning into everyday action. They challenge them to practice skills like leading meetings, handling conflicts, heading up and staffing projects, motivating people, troubleshooting, and problem-solving. They put them in touch with other coaches, mentors, and supporters throughout the organization who can accelerate their learning curve. They send an important message throughout their organizations: Leadership development is the accountability of every supervisory manager.

By the "next generation of leaders," we generally refer to Gen Xers and older Gen Yers, who will constitute the prime-age workforce for the next five to 15 years. However, we don't want to dismiss those Schwarzkopfers and Boomers who are also eager to assume leadership positions.

For example, we met a sixtysomething who, because of family obligations, had only been in the workforce for 10 years. She told us she was now qualified and willing to become a manager, but her organization only promoted younger people. Or take the fiftysomething who said now that her children were in high school, she'd enjoy the travel and responsibilities that come with a leadership position.

Our advice? Don't miss opportunities to capitalize on older workers, too, and their maturity and experience, when you're scouting for leadership talent.

Once these seasoned managers develop new leaders, they don't hoard them; they willingly export them wherever they're needed throughout the organization. The payoff for these savvy managers? A reputation for leadership development that makes talented people want to work with them, and a network of protégés throughout the organization who expand their span of influence.

Turn Urgency Into Opportunity

You know there's a leadership crisis in your organization. If you're responsible for too many direct reports, too many projects, too many clients, you're bearing the brunt of it right now. A sure-fire way to relieve the pressure on you—as well as to ensure solid leadership bench strength for your organization—is to make leadership development a top priority during your day-to-day interactions with your staff.

How do you to do that? Throughout our research, we've discovered the most cost-effective, productive way to produce new leaders is to hold yourself accountable for two major competencies:

1. Becoming a leadership scout who is constantly on the lookout for high-potential candidates and who recruits them into a customized leadership development program

2. Becoming a leadership coach who helps candidates identify their strengths and skill gaps, finds resources and other supportive relationships to help them accelerate their learning curve, and puts them into ad hoc leadership roles to test their leadership talent and skills quickly and easily

I. Becoming a Leadership Talent Scout

Scouting for leadership talent requires using a new lens through which to observe your direct reports' character, talents, skills, and motivation. Starting today, observe every person explicitly through the leadership lens, considering each one a possible candidate until that individual is ruled out. As you rule him or her out, don't be troubled. It is not fair to treat everybody the same if everybody is not the same. It is perfectly fair to identify high performers who meet certain leadership standards and to reward them with special development efforts. Those whom you rule out are not being punished; they are simply not being selected for leadership development.

Who's Out?

While some of the following may seem obvious, we've seen organizations promote people to management positions despite obvious red flags. Typically they want to believe that a problem is minor and can be overlooked if they focus on more promising indicators of a person's success. Our research, however, shows that these red flags are clear warning signs of trouble ahead. The following five in particular merit concern:

1. Any consistent performance or behavior problem. This includes chronic lateness, failure to meet goals and deadlines, and disregard for the policies of the organization.

2. Lack of interest in the mission. Without a strong commitment to the mission of the organization and the team, a manager can't inspire and motivate others.

3. Ethical lapses. Recent employee surveys indicate that honesty, integrity, and ethics are the most desirable attributes of a leader. Therefore, those who have a record of lying, cheating, stealing, verbal abuse, physical abuse, abuse of property, or a lack of respect for others should be ruled out.

4. "I, me, mine" thinking. Those who think, speak, and act primarily out of self-interest and rarely consider the best interests of the team or organization should be ruled out.

5. Coaching-resistance. Those who don't respond positively to constructive feedback and coaching

are unfit for leadership. We've discovered that even "A" list high producers probably won't make effective leaders if they themselves are uncoachable.

When such red flags appear, your best bet is to cross those people off your leadership list immediately.

Who's In?

Hundreds of leadership books describing thousands of characteristics and skills are published every year. We've narrowed the focus down to 10 major skills that most experts agree are baseline for leadership and management. Use these as green flags for your scouting guide:

1. Initiative. Does this person recognize opportunities and problems and then take appropriate action to achieve concrete results without specific direction?

2. Strategic thinking. Does this person have an ability to look at both the big picture and the details—the forest and the trees?

3. Strategic learning. Does this person regularly anticipate his or her skill and knowledge gaps and fill those gaps in a timely and appropriate fashion?

4. Communication. Does this person take responsibility for building strong interpersonal relationships on the team? Does this person actively listen and have the ability to express his or her thoughts effectively, both in the spoken and written word?

5. Problem solving. Does this person give up easily when faced with problems, or stick with a problem until it is solved or until the damage from the problem is minimized as much as possible? Does he or she ask, "How can we do this?" rather than, "Can we do this?"

6. Creativity. Does this person recognize that there are numerous right answers to most questions? Is he or she willing to take risks and engage in trial and error? Is this person willing and able to test solutions that may seem illogical, impractical, against the "rules"? Is this person comfortable with ambiguity? Does this person have lots of original ideas?

7. Ability to motivate. Does this individual set an example of high performance that others seem to imitate? Does he or she celebrate the success of others and help people learn from their failures? Does this individual have "fans" among his or her coworkers, managers, vendors, or customers?

8. Team building. Does this person genuinely like working with people and working through the challenges they offer? Does this person have an appreciation for others, including those who are different from him or her? Does this person create an environment of mutual trust among team members? Does this person delegate significant responsibility to others and give others credit for their contributions? Do others enthusiastically follow his or her lead?

9. Project management. If this person has already had experience leading projects, how effective are

his or her skills of planning, staffing, documenting progress, troubleshooting, and coaching individuals on the team? If the person hasn't had firsthand experience yet, what ad hoc opportunities can you offer immediately so you can accurately evaluate his or her current skill level?

10. People management. If this individual already has supervisory responsibility, how effective are his or her skills of goal setting, providing feedback, customizing rewards, and handling performance issues? If the individual has not had supervisory experience yet, what ad hoc opportunities can you offer immediately so you can accurately evaluate his or her current skill level?

This is only a partial list of skills. Your job is to take our list and refine it so it reflects the expectations your organization has of its managers/leaders. Even if your candidates lack some skills, everyone can succeed if they have the willingness to learn and work hard to improve. Therefore, strongly consider anyone on your team who holds several green flags for your management development program.

Recruit Candidates in Your Management Development Program

Once you have identified a potential new leader, your next challenge is to engage that person in a "recruiting" conversation. Make an appointment and prepare to carry out the following process:

1. Explain your purpose to the individual: that you have identified him or her as a high-potential candidate for leadership. Make sure it's understood that this is not a selection for a promotion or a fast-track program. Share

what you've observed through daily activities that has led you to believe the person has management potential. Be specific about the times, places, situations, and people involved, and the leadership characteristics and skills exhibited by the person.

2. Explain what your commitment will entail during the management development process. For example, you'll help evaluate the candidate's leadership and management skills. You'll concentrate your time and resources on training, tracking the person's progress, assisting in building developmental relationships, steering ad hoc leadership opportunities in the person's direction, and coaching him or her along the way.

   Given the desire of Gen Xers and Yers to learn market-able skills (and the Boomer drive for improvement), your commitment to provide help is a major selling point.

3. Explain what you expect from the candidate in return: commitment to the challenges of management develop-ment, participation in charting his or her own path to management, and determination to set an example of working hard, learning well, and growing in competency.

4. If you gain that commitment, engage the candidate in an initial self-assessment based on your green flags so the learning process can begin immediately. Let the person know you will be offering him or her your own evaluation and will solicit others from managers and coworkers with whom the person has worked closely in the past.

   Be aware that self-evaluation is one of the most difficult yet useful skills you can teach emerging leaders. Since the word "development" means an unfolding, make sure candidates understand that they're embarking on the process of unfolding talents and skills in a supportive environment and strengthening them through on-the-job practice. Your only expectation at this point is that candidates have the talent and the willingness to learn, practice, and grow through the process. And the only way to embark on leadership "unfolding" is to know clearly where skill and knowledge strengths and gaps lie. Therefore, rigorous honesty is non-negotiable on every self-evaluation.

5. Create a tracking system that will document each candidate's ongoing progress from current levels of expertise to desired levels of expertise.

Once you've identified and enrolled your leadership candidates, you can don the hat of leadership coach and begin finding resources, supportive relationships, and ad hoc roles to develop their talent and skills.

2. Becoming a Leadership Coach

Start developing this second required competency by preparing to carry out the following five-step process:

1. Identify the development resources already available in your organization. They include:

   • Formal internal classroom and/or online training

   • Formal external classroom and/or online training provided by colleges/universities, industry accreditation groups, or outside training vendors

- Informal internal training in the form short-term projects, coaching, or mentoring from knowledgeable individuals

- Informal external training received through volunteer work, research, membership in professional associations, and professional reading

2. Calculate the costs involved in any learning opportunities, the time commitment required for the learning, and the time you are willing to allocate to your new leader. Also factor in any approvals you must obtain from HR or your manager before you proceed.

3. Ask leadership candidates to create their own learning plans based on their strengths as well as their skill gaps. Be sure to identify all the training resources you've uncovered and the time you're offering them to use those resources.

   Just as self-evaluation is an essential skill for leadership development, so is creating strategic learning plans based on the individual's identified goals. Asking candidates to implement a learning plan without getting them involved in creating it is counterproductive. Our research finds that unless a person is learning-ready, the best-designed plans won't work. To ensure that readiness, put the locus of control for creating the learning plan in the individual's hands.

4. Hold each leadership candidate accountable for building a transferable skills portfolio. Holding candidates accountable puts the locus of success in their hands.

Once a new leader begins to execute the learning plan, make sure that he or she gathers proof of completion of each learning opportunity.

5. Periodically schedule a new self-evaluation and a new manager-evaluation. Documentation of increased proficiency in each skill will make up the emerging leader's portfolio.

Finding Supporters for Your Emerging Leaders

Developmental relationships are critical to the unfolding of leadership talent. Of course, one of the most important relationships your management candidates have is with you. But you are not enough. You can't possibly do all the work necessary to create great managers, nor is it fair to place that accountability totally on your shoulders. In fact, it takes a village of professionals to do the job well. Therefore, your emerging leaders need to establish multiple relationships throughout the organization to gain leadership skills, wisdom, and experience more quickly and thoroughly. A main part of your job as a leadership coach is to help them do that.

Take a look at five professional relationships that will accelerate their development:

1. **Coaching-style managers.** Encourage your new leaders to seek out other coaching-style managers and help them get assigned to challenging projects with those managers to sharpen specific management skills. Who can enhance their team-building skills, their creativity skills, their communication skills? Help

emerging leaders find the best coach for their strengths and learning gaps, and help them forge mutually productive relationships.

2. **Personal coaches.** Personal coaches help individuals work on specific personal or professional issues that interfere with their ability to grow and excel. They are objective third parties who can be bluntly honest about issues of personality, style, habit, or practice that must be changed if a new leader is going to reach his or her potential. Personal coaching is expensive and is usually reserved for senior executives. But you should go to bat to get funds to hire a personal coach for a promising leadership candidate if you think it appropriate—and if the candidate's worth to the organization is crystal clear.

3. **Mentors.** The concept of mentoring is commonly misunderstood. Often organizations engage in initiatives whereby more experienced individuals are matched with less experienced individuals and these relationships are called mentoring. Our view is that mentoring doesn't happen overnight. It takes months or even years to develop a true mentoring relationship. How do you support mentorship? First, recruit would-be mentors and find ways to teach them the basics of mentoring. Second, teach would-be protégés the basics of building a relationship with a mentor and growing in that kind of relationship.

4. **Organizational supporters.** These are people in the organization with influence and authority who take an interest in one or more emerging leaders and go out of their way to support those leaders as fully as possible. Who in your organization likes to get behind young leaders and build them up by steering them toward formal and informal learning opportunities, relationship

opportunities, creative challenges, stretch goals, high-profile assignments, and other support? How can you make those organizational supporters familiar with one or more emerging leaders? How can you make those organizational supporters committed to building up those emerging leaders?

5. **Boards of Directors.** Some of your emerging leaders may be willing to do the extensive work of recruiting and maintaining their own personal "board of directors," a group of experienced people in a variety of disciplines who would be willing to help them speed up their learning curve. Based on your experience, who could you recommend for this board? Rather than hoping that one solid mentoring relationship will develop over time, steer your leaders toward this broader approach and help them identify the short-term goals they want to achieve with each person. Of course, it will take a lot of work on both sides to make this something that is meaningful and enduring.

Remember, it's inappropriate for you to mentor someone for whom you have immediate supervisory responsibility. However, after you develop and export new leaders to roles outside your scope of authority, you may redefine your relationship and become their mentor. For now, discuss mentoring with your emerging leaders as a two-way proposition: They have as much accountability as the mentor for defining, co-designing, and maintaining the relationship as well as ensuring that it becomes mutually beneficial.

 Note: For more on creating mentoring relationships, see Chapter 11.

Propelling Emerging Leaders Into Ad Hoc Roles

How do you consistently test, monitor, coach, and develop your emerging leaders' talents, skills, and traits? The most practical way is through engaging them in ad hoc leadership opportunities.

What are ad hoc leadership opportunities? Those opportunities not reflected on the organization chart or requiring a formal promotion. They are short-term projects aligned with the goals of your team or department. They test your new leader's project and people management skills, and offer him or her the challenges of a leadership role. They become personal case studies, allowing both of you to identify strengths and improvement areas more realistically.

As a leadership coach, you now have real-time situations from which to measure and monitor progress. And, most important, you have on-the-job opportunities to help you develop your leadership bench strength more quickly. This investment ultimately produces people who will relieve you of some of your own management pressures.

To provide your emerging leaders with ad hoc leadership opportunities, consider the following steps:

1. Be on the lookout for short-term projects that align with the particular skills and experience of each new leader.

2. Once you've found a project, work with the new leader in preparing for the role and the work involved. Help the person to . . .

    •   Use project management skills to identify goals, deadlines, parameters, and guidelines

- Sharpen people management skills by recruiting the best people for the team, identifying the role each team member will play, and gaining commitment from each member for specific goals, tasks, and deadlines

3. Ensure the new leader has sufficient authority within the team to carry out his or her role effectively. Serve as a PR person by assigning and supporting that authority at the beginning of the project.

4. Once the project begins, coach the new leader at regular intervals along the way. Schedule formal check-in times to debrief the project's progress and to discuss any unforeseen challenges the leader is experiencing. Also, let him or her know you are available for informal conversations if and when they are needed.

5. Require the new leader to keep a running list of lessons learned. Since the purpose of this ad hoc opportunity is development—the "unfolding" of leadership skills—documenting such things as successes, stumbling blocks, questions, and gaps in skill or knowledge is essential.

6. Document your own list of lessons learned. This is a leadership development opportunity for you as well. How well did you prepare your emerging leader for the project? How effectively did you coach him or her during its execution? What could you have done differently? What could you do better next time?

7. Finally, conduct a thorough debriefing after the project's completion. Do your homework in advance. Interview team members. Evaluate the results. Study your own list of lessons learned. This is a tremendous opportunity for

stretch learning—for both you and your emerging leader. It's an opportunity to revisit the leadership skills analysis you conducted earlier, when scouting talent, and to assess the new leader's progress. It's also a prime opportunity to examine this person's emerging leadership style and practices.

Learning to Let Go

After investing a substantial amount of time and energy in identifying and developing a new leader, you may find that letting the person go is too difficult a directive to follow. But that is exactly what you must do. Having developed a valuable team member who now can share the burden of managing people, you must resist the temptation to hoard his or her leadership talent as your own. Your final challenge, then, is becoming known for your expertise in exporting new leaders.

What's in it for the new leader? Career opportunities. What's in it for the organization? New leadership talent and bench strength. What's in it for you? Two invaluable benefits:

- A network of protégés with growing influence and authority whom you will likely call upon throughout the rest of your career

- A reputation for growing leaders

Your track record is likely to be rewarded as the organization reaps the benefits of your development skills. Being known as a leadership scout, coach, and exporter also means that talented employees will request to work with you. You will inevitably attract great people to your team, giving you access to the best and brightest contributors.

As emphasized in Part One of this book, Gen Xers and Yers demand options and opportunities to amass marketable skills if they are going to continue to commit their time, energy, and talent to your organization. What better way to retain the most talented among them than for you, their manager, to become their leadership coach, engaging them in just-in-time development opportunities that capitalize on their talents and skills?

Strategic Imperatives to Head Off Your Leadership Crisis

If you hold a senior management position, consider analyzing your current leadership-management needs immediately. Follow the steps and ask the questions provided in the guidelines sheet that concludes this chapter, and share your findings with managers across the organization.

If you're not in senior management, recommend these guidelines to the appropriate people in authority. Let them know you are aware of the urgent need to address the leadership crisis in your organization today, given the shrinking pool of leadership candidates to come. Make the case that those organizations who seize opportunities to recruit and develop leadership talent now will be able to pass the leadership mantle to the next generation more quickly and easily.

Guidelines:
Analyzing Current Leadership Needs

Steps:

1. Working with HR, gather data about your current leadership-management "state of the union."

2. Engage your managers in studying this staffing data. Use focus groups, surveys, and/or interviews to find out where the leadership hot spots are.

3. Finally, define and implement concrete actions you must take to address your leadership needs.

Questions to Ask:

- What does our current data reveal about leadership gaps now? What does it forecast for the near future?

- What are our present approaches to leadership development? Which actually result in more leadership competency and bench strength?

- Which of our managers will be retiring within the next three to five years? What is our succession plan with them? What is our knowledge transfer strategy?

- Which of our current managers are legitimately overburdened and will need some relief? By when?

- Which managers could get that relief if they were trained to get faster, better, smarter work from their team or department?

- Which managers need development opportunities in order to become leadership scouts and coaches?

- Which managers are naturally leadership scouts and coaches and can serve as teachers?

- What suggestions do current managers have to get themselves up to speed on scouting and coaching?

- How would those managers prefer to be recognized and rewarded for developing and exporting emerging leaders?

Chapter II

Managing Your Parents—or Grandparents: You're in Good Company

A Case Study:
The Ninja Assassin and the Wingman

WHEN CARTER DURYEA, the 26-year-old rising star in the film *In Good Company,* gets promoted to advertising sales manager at a sports magazine, his exuberant reaction is, "I'm going to kick butt and take no prisoners . . . I'm going to be a ninja assassin!"

Underneath this bravado, however, is a scared Gen Yer who has no idea what he's doing. Coming face to face with 51-year-old Dan Freeman, the former manager who is older than his father, Carter keeps up his ninja façade. He admits he has no experience but is a fast learner, and then arrogantly informs Dan that he has "the potential to be an awesome wingman." When Dan asks, "What's the benefit for me?" Carter smugly responds, "You get to keep your job."

Carter Duryea is the product of youthful ambition plus early success minus the benefits of hard-earned experience. While smart enough to keep Freeman on as a "wingman"— the "old guy" knows more about the business than he ever will—Carter is clueless about leading meetings, creating teams, and maintaining client relationships. He's also so self-absorbed that he can't see his own name being written on the proverbial wall until it's too late.

In the end, fortunes reverse: Dan wins back his manager's seat and Carter, his own butt dramatically kicked, is backed out into the cold. However, the chastened Gen Yer walks away from this experience a wiser young man. His closing remark to Dan is genuine: "No one took the time to give me a hard time before, to teach me what was worth knowing."

One can hope this energetic, talented, ambitious young man—and those of his ilk—will have the wisdom to seek out other older professionals to test his mettle, give him a hard time, and teach him what is worth knowing. If he does, he will, indeed, remain in good company.

Reflected by Art: A New Workplace Trend

In Good Company reflects a real-life workplace trend: More young men and women are managing more older workers than ever before. This trend dovetails with the much larger shift away from traditional sources of authority—seniority, age, experience, rank—providing more opportunities for twenty- and thirtysomethings to manage forty-, fifty- and sixtysomethings.

For older workers, the prospect of being supervised by someone young enough to be their child (or grandchild) is as disconcerting as managing people old enough to be parents (or grandparents) is daunting. Although the focus of this chapter is how younger managers can succeed with older workers, we won't resist the temptation to offer a few suggestions to those Schwarzkopfers and Boomers managed by Xers or Yers. Both sides of the desk have major adjustments to make in this new workplace relationship.

Initial Challenges: Our Advice to Gen Xers and Yers in Management

First of all, you need to remember: You *are* young and probably have much less experience than those you manage, so don't be insulted if your direct reports know that too. Your initial challenge is to prove that you're appropriate to the task—without being a ninja assassin. How do you do that? Essentially, make sure you're not setting yourself up to be treated like a "kid." You don't have to be serious, but you do have to take your role and responsibilities seriously. Step back and ask yourself:

- What messages am I sending through my clothes, my grooming, my body language, my tone of voice?

- How does my verbal language affect my credibility?

Ask a trusted colleague to give you honest feedback about the image you project at meetings, on the phone, through your written correspondence. What unconscious habits can you tweak so you're not sabotaged by behaviors that keep you "a kid" in older workers' eyes?

Second, remember that your staffers may be just as uneasy as you are. Many are not thrilled by the prospect of being managed by someone young enough to be their child or grandchild. So, right away, you have common ground for a great conversation. Clear the air immediately and have a good chuckle about the parent/child comparison, and then get on with it. The last thing anyone wants to hear all the time is how he or she reminds you of your dad or mom, son or daughter.

Of course, you may have to be courageous enough to have a difficult conversation with someone who continuously treats you like a kid. He or she may just be testing your mettle, so pass the test by clearly defining how you want others to treat you. This goes to the heart of your credibility as a manager. You are, after all, the person your organization entrusted to lead this team.

Once you have met these initial challenges, continue to build credibility as a manager who takes charge and does what's right. This means holding yourself accountable for developing into a high-performance manager who holds his or her people accountable for high performance. This is a long-term commitment—becoming an expert manager takes more than a promotion or a few months' experience—but you can prove by your actions *now* that you're determined to do your best for the organization and for your team. Our further advice in this chapter will help you do that.

Seven Strategies for Developing "Best Practice" Management Habits

Because you're comparatively new to the profession of management, you probably haven't acquired too many bad management habits yet. That's to your advantage. Your task is to make conscious choices of the skills, techniques, and best practices that will define your management style and earn you the respect of every team member of every age. What are some of those conscious choices that you must turn into solid management habits? Consider the following seven strategies.

1. Find Out Where Each Team Member Is Coming From

Take the time to get to know every person on your team. Figure out where each is coming from in terms of experience, knowledge, and skills. Whose expertise and wisdom can help you succeed? Find at least one wise sage on your team, someone who can tell you the inside scoop and advise you on resources, pitfalls, shortcuts, and contexts. If you can, find someone to be your own Dan Freeman: the person who will take the time to give you a hard time and teach you what's worth knowing. Let that person know you will value any mentoring or coaching he or she can offer to make you a better manager. Just don't overdo it. Afterall, you are the manager.

2. Find Out Where Each Team Member Is Going

Discover where everyone is going in terms of their desire to learn new skills, have new experiences, try new tasks, advance their career, or plan for retirement. Assure them that you consider it one of your primary responsibilities to help them remain productive contributors who find satisfaction in their work (a Schwarzkopfer imperative) and who are continually challenged to keep growing and learning in their own way (a Boomer imperative).

3. Pay Attention to Personal Working Styles

Learn as much as you can about everyone's individual working style: How do they prefer to communicate (e.g., email, face to face, daily, weekly)? How frequently and in what format do they want your feedback? Do they prefer daily or weekly goals and deadlines? Are they

---

Preparing for Your Meetings: Suggested Multigenerational Review

---

Before you conduct one-on-one meetings with your staffers, review the first four chapters of this book to refresh your memory of each generation's current needs and expectations. This will give you a context for some of the attitudes and values you'll hear expressed during your conversations.

Also, review the management best practices we recommend. As you work more closely with each person, you'll be able to discern the most effective ones to use. That said, cut yourself some slack here because much of management is trial-and-error. Even the most seasoned managers who try to figure out what approach works best with what people don't always get it right the first time around.

---

morning people or afternoon people? What else do you need to know to create a mutually advantageous working relationship with them?

To receive team feedback on your feedback and to gauge how well you're learning about working styles, consider using the questionnaire on the next page. We offer this form to managers in our training programs to help them provide coaching-style feedback—a key communication skill for any manager. Give each team member a copy of the form; then either schedule one-on-one interviews to discuss the answers or ask members to respond via email. Make sure you report to the entire team on the results— the good, bad, and ugly—and announce your specific commitments to improve over the next three to six months. Ask the team to help you keep those commitments.

Questionnaire:
Help Me Give You Better Feedback

Directions: Please answer the following questions fully and honestly. Everyone on our team has received this questionnaire and I will report the results to the entire team.

1. Do you feel that you need, in general, more feedback or less feedback than I currently give you? Are there certain tasks, responsibilities, or projects for which you need more feedback than usual? Less feedback than usual?

2. How do you generally prefer to receive feedback? In writing? In person? By voice mail? By email? Are there certain tasks, responsibilities, or projects for which you have different preferences?

3. What time of the day are you busiest? Least busy? What is generally the best time for me to give you feedback? Are there certain tasks, responsibilities, or projects for which you have different preferences?

4. Are you clear on your goals or next steps after I give you feedback? If not, what are some ways I could clarify them?

5. Do I balance praise and criticism? Do I over-praise or over-criticize? If so, when does this happen?

6. Do I seem to put thought into feedback? Do I make false assumptions, or act on incorrect information? If so, how can I check my facts so that this doesn't happen?

7. Do I follow up on feedback after I give it to make sure you're back on track or moving ahead? If not, what would be the best time for me to follow up with you?

4. Become a Take-Charge Leader

Avoid the bad habit of those old-style managers who only talked to their people when things went wrong. Instead, take charge and make work-related conversations with your people a management imperative. Rain or shine, triumphs or mistakes, hold a one-on-one meeting at least once a week with each team member. Focus your time on their work: goals, deadlines, resource needs, promises, and commitments. To get started, see our easy-to-use meeting agenda in Chapter 7, Best Practice 9.

Gradually, you'll discover what you need to talk about, how you need to talk with each person, and what kind of tracking system you both need to document your conversations.

5. Use Intervention When Needed

As you become knowledgeable about the work each team member does, have the guts to intervene when anyone's performance slips below acceptable levels. Hold performance improvement conversations focused on what a person needs to do to keep his or her job, and be prepared to let hopelessly low performers go, whatever their age. Like any other manager, you must come to terms with the resentment that high performers feel toward low performers—they end up doing low performers' work but not getting their pay. Realize that you will sabotage your own credibility as a take-charge manager if you allow low performers to hang around.

Be aware that you may have inherited some staffers who were either allowed "to coast" by inept managers or hired under one set of expectations but ask to perform under another. For example, a nursing manager told us she recently fired a 20-year veteran nurse who wouldn't buy into their hospital's new customer-service commitment. Because this nurse had been willing to work night shifts for two decades, she was considered a valuable asset. However, as complaints from patients and coworkers about her negative attitude escalated, this asset became a liability. Working nights no longer gave her the leeway to treat people unprofessionally. Since she refused to adapt to the new customer-service expectations, she had to go.

6. Become a Coaching-Style Manager Who Facilitates Results

Rather than dictating results, facilitate them—just make sure the process for achieving those results is clear. (If you're unfamiliar with the most effective processes, tap your experienced members for their expertise.) In particular, your older workers need a "boss" whose approach is to focus everyone on the game plan—the team's mission and goals—and to ensure they have the direction, support, and resources they need to do their jobs very well. Review Chapter 6 and think about implementing some of the best practices suggested there.

One sure-fire way to earn staffers' respect is to let them know you are willing to jump through hoops, cut red tape, and go to bat for them to obtain what they need in order to do their jobs well. When they succeed and are recognized for their work by both you and the organization, they'll love you, no matter how young you are.

7. Reward People for High Performance

Gain a reputation as the manager who rewards people for high performance, on both an individual and a team level. The sooner you discover what lights each person's fire, the sooner you can begin to negotiate custom deals and offer incentives to recognize and drive high performance. Refer to Chapter 8 for ideas about the most sought-after incentives, and engage your team members in the brainstorming exercise we suggest in Best Practice 22. Let everyone know what's on the table and make customized incentives part of your ongoing dialogue with each person.

Other Sources of Credibility

Here are more suggestions to help you build your managerial credibility with a multigenerational team.

- **Take a course in presentation skills.** Whether you're running a small group meeting or addressing a large group of professionals, few skills enhance your credibility faster than presentation skills. As one seasoned pro reminded a younger colleague, "If you can think on your feet, you can think in your seat. Public-speaking skills are valuable in and of themselves, but there's added value: They'll make it so much easier for you have those uncomfortable one-on-one meetings."

- **Become an expert listener.** One of the best ways to show people respect is through listening—whether to a Schwarzkopfer who's concerned about retirement or a Gen Y looking for the next career opportunity. Gain a reputation for being a genuinely caring listener.

- **Keep your promises.** Be careful what you promise people. Be thoughtful about the commitments you make. One easy way to lose credibility is not to deliver on your word.

➡

Other Sources of Credibility (concluded)

- **Avoid "nice-itis."** Some managers think they should spare people's feelings by being "nice" about substandard performance or behavior. But letting poor performers assume they're doing well is not being "nice"; it's being deceptive—and does a disservice to them, other team members, and your organization. Always be clear about your expectations and worker commitments and accountabilities; then, take the time to give substandard performers a hard time. Remember, the opposite of being nice is not being nasty; it's being truthful. This will take courage, but will earn you credibility.

- **Commit to your own ongoing training.** Consider training in industry-related and management-related areas. If you're on the cutting edge of your profession, people will notice. Your credibility depends on that as well as on your leadership competency. Let people know you are committed to lifelong learning.

- **Become an active member of professional associations.** Networking with industry professionals outside your organization gives you access to a reservoir of experience, expertise, perspectives, and innovative ideas that can only enrich your team. Also, volunteer to head up projects and committees to develop your leadership skills and gain visibility within the professional community.

- **Write articles for your organization's or industry's newsletters.** Whether you're touting the accomplishments of your team or reporting on an innovative business solution, getting your name in print is a credibility enhancer. Tap your team members for ideas and recognize them in print, too.

Becoming the Worthy Protégé of a Worthy Mentor

In addition to the strategies above, you can enhance your management credibility by becoming the worthy protégé of a worthy mentor—or of a mosaic of mentors. What is a mentor? A mentor is an accomplished, experienced, wise person willing to spend time with and teach another person who is less accomplished, experienced, and wise. A mentor does all the following:

- Walks a path you want to follow

- Sets an example you can imitate

- Teaches and shares experiences

- Answers your difficult questions and asks even more difficult ones

- Pushes you and demands more of you than you demand of yourself

- Believes you are capable of achieving the impossible and is willing to help you achieve it

- Provides you with unique opportunities to prove yourself

- Values your opinions and ideas by seeking your input and learning from you

- Likes you, cares about you, and even loves you

Most successful professionals will tell you that having a mentor was a major key to their success. Don't wait until you *think* you need a mentor: You already do—that's a given. Start searching outside your team and department for one—or several—right now.

Where, precisely, do you find a mentor? That depends on what you want to learn, but the field of possible mentors is wide open. Perhaps a family member fits the description of a mentor, or perhaps a retiree, customer, vendor, professor, professional association colleague, or community leader. Whom do you know reasonably well, respect, and wish to emulate?

Wherever you look, understand that mentoring is a two-way proposition: You have as much accountability as the mentor for defining, designing, and maintaining the relationship and for ensuring that the relationship becomes mutually beneficial. In the best situations, the mentor receives as much benefit as his or her protégé.

Mastering Protégé Skills

One of most powerful factors in building a mutually beneficial mentoring relationship is your ability and willingness to master protégé skills. These skills are essential for attracting relationships, thriving in them, and convincing mentors to continue to help you succeed. The following process will help you develop three skill essentials.

1. Select people you admire and trust. Discerning who has the characteristics and track record to merit admiration and trust is a prerequisite for defining a good mentor— and a protégé skill. Make an initial list of people who qualify for your admiration and trust. Ask:

- What have they done, said, and accomplished to merit admiration and trust?

- What feedback about them can you glean from other professionals you trust?

- Do they have the time to mentor?

- Are they willing to enter into this type of relationship with a younger person?

2. Define what you want from a mentoring relationship and set concrete goals to achieve it. Prepare answers to the following questions and discuss them with a potential mentor at an initial meeting:

- What do I want to receive from this mentorship relationship?

- What goals do I have in mind?

- How frequently would I like to meet face to face or speak on the phone?

- How will we define the purpose of each meeting or phone call?

- How will we measure the success of our relationship?

- How will we know we've reached the limit of the effectiveness of our relationship and need to move on?

Being clear on what you want, and setting intermediate goals that will help you achieve it, is also a protégé skill.

3. Be open to using the mentor's ongoing feedback to grow in knowledge and wisdom. Consider the following story:

There was a young karate student who practiced very hard and was highly skilled. When his teacher died, he searched and searched, until he finally found a master with whom he wanted to continue his studies. He visited the master and asked to be accepted as a new student. To demonstrate his worth, and thus impress the master, he showed off his best skills, his finest techniques, almost every trick he had in his repertoire.

After hours of watching this performance, the master invited the student to sit down for a cup of tea. The master set out two teacups, filled his own first, and then began filling the student's cup. The tea reached the cup's rim, and still the master kept pouring. It ran over the rim, and still the master kept pouring, letting the tea spill over the table and onto the floor. The student jumped to his feet, exclaiming, "My cup is too full! My cup is too full!" The master nodded sagely and said, "Yes. Your cup is too full. Come back when your cup is empty. Then you will have room for my teachings."

Before establishing a mentoring relationship, you need to empty your cup to make room for a mentor's "teachings." Being able to do that can prove the most difficult of our protégé skills. Are you ready to develop this skill?

Final Thoughts for Young Managers

If you're a Gen Xer or Gen Yer who has accepted a position of authority in your organization, congratulations.

You are a member of the next generation of leaders who will lead businesses well into the twenty-first century—and workers of all ages need you to succeed. As we said in the introduction to this book, it is harder to manage people today than ever before, so you have your work cut out for you. However, if you focus on the essential skills, techniques, and practices that the best managers today use to lead multigenerational teams, you will be well on your way.

Our Advice to Schwarzkopfers and Boomers

Okay, it's happened. Don't be insulted by the situation. Let go of your ego and accept your new young manager. Remember, your organization may have promoted the young upstart to try something new. Don't be the one digging in your heels and refusing to go along with change. To help you through this generational transition in leadership, here are several other "kernels" of advice:

- Assess, but do not test, your young manager. As with any manager, determine whether this individual can help you contribute, succeed, and gain rewards in the workplace. If not, you should plan your exit strategy, as would be advisable with any manager.

- If you must talk about "it," talk about it once. Then drop it. The last thing your new manager wants is a staffer who plays parent. What most young people in management roles value is to be taken seriously and earn your respect. They've had enough parental controls at home and certainly don't want to bump into them at work. So don't keep reminding them they remind you of your son or daughter. You may mean it as a compliment, but it won't be taken that way.

- Be the wise sage, the "wingman" or "wingwoman." If you think your young manager lacks experience, context, and wisdom, then be the one to offer some. But offer your advice in private and be careful not to overdo it. Many young people want to try things on their own, make a few mistakes, take risks, and come out having learned valuable lessons. Be vigilant for those situations when your advice would be truly appreciated, or simply wait to be asked for help. And once again, don't play parent.

- Learn as much as you can about the young manager's management style, understanding that it is a work in progress. How does this person like to communicate (e.g., email, face to face, daily, weekly)? How frequently will the manager discuss goals and deadlines with you and provide feedback?

- Make sure you clearly communicate your needs and expectations. Even the most seasoned managers are not mind readers. Position yourself as someone who is there to help the entire team have satisfying, productive, fun experiences at work.

- Be great at managing yourself. Get lots of work done very well, very fast, one day after another. Position yourself as a creative problem-solver rather than a hard-nosed problem-creator.

- Finally, enjoy the energy, eagerness, and freshness this young person has to offer you and your team. He or she may well be the very person who provides you with the flexible work arrangements, opportunities for new experiences, and recognition and reward you deserve as you wind down your career with this organization and plan for the next stages of your life.

Chapter 12

Teaching Teens How to Serve Your Customers: How Well Are You Doing?

THE LAST MULTIGENERATIONAL OPPORTUNITY at your disposal has to do with young Gen Yers and the most valuable skill set any business can teach them: customer service. Since young workers are disproportionately represented in frontline customer service positions, and study after study shows that customers complain most often about this generation's service inability, we wanted to find out what managers were doing to prepare the next generation of workers to become customer service experts.

We talked with high school students working part-time in customer service jobs, as well as college students who remembered what it was like to be "the new kid" on the block. These older Gen Yers added the perspective of full-time work experience and offered practical suggestions about the customer service training they would have liked to receive earlier in their careers.

From what both groups report, the news for managers is not good. These Yers give most managers very low grades when it comes to customer service training.

For example, consider the hardware store manager in the Midwest who had just hired 11 teens. "I can't believe them," he complained. "They trample customers on their way to the back room to do inventory. None of them ever stops to help a customer. I sure don't need 11 kids in the back. Why won't they help my customers?"

When we asked him to describe the customer service training he offered his new hires, his response was a quizzical expression. He hadn't thought to tell them that the reason they were hired in the first place was to serve his customers. He hadn't provided them with opportunities to shadow his current service pros or helped them to engage in role-plays on handling difficult people. He hadn't set up ongoing education on his products so they could confidently talk with customers. When young people don't know that becoming a customer service expert is a top priority—and they haven't been trained to act like one—doing inventory in a back room makes sense. Who wants to do be embarrassed or look dumb in front of customers?

This manager isn't alone. One of the biggest mistakes companies make is to hire young workers, give them little or no training, and then reprimand them when they don't perform well. A 19-year-old sales associate in a retail store reported, "I actually started working the same day I was hired. They threw me out on the floor and said, 'Just watch and learn.' I didn't receive proper training until the fourth month I worked there. [In the meantime,] I was written up three times for not assisting customers."

Three Strikes for Teens

It's one thing to learn how to flip burgers, stock clothing racks, or bag groceries. It's another to deal professionally with people of all ages with different needs, demands, and emotional baggage.

Adults admit that delivering excellent customer service consistently is one of the most challenging tasks they face at work every day. How much harder, then, for younger Gen Yers whose age and limited experience often put them at a distinct disadvantage. As an 18-year-old lifeguard explained, "[Older] customers won't follow rules or listen to instructions from me. I think because I'm young, they don't respect me. They think that they don't need me there telling them what to do."

In this area, adult assumptions about younger Gen Yers amount to three strikes for these teens:

- **Strike one.** Young Gen Yers are often perceived as too young to have any authority or know very much about anything except video games, snowboarding, or mall hopping. A 17-year-old bank teller confided that she finally removed her "High School Trainee" badge because customers demanded she count and re-count their money. As soon as she did, the demands stopped.

- **Strike two.** Some adults assume that young Gen Yers don't need training in the interpersonal skills necessary to deliver great customer service. "It's just common sense," managers say. "They should smile, be polite, and give the customer what the customer wants." But common sense is uncommon in any generation. As one teen confided, her bakery store manager preaches that "the customer is God, treat them like VIPs . . . and yet he yells at me in front of them." A 19-year-old waiter added, "A lot of my managers have not had [customer service] training themselves, or rarely utilize it during work hours." So much for common sense.

Granted, some Yers have been involved in customer service work since they were 15 years old and are smart enough to learn through observation. Or, they've been lucky enough to have helpful coworkers to field their questions. However, relying on observation and luck is not the most effective way to train the emerging workforce.

• **Strike three.** Some adults assume that because young people are techno-savvy, they are business savvy. Consequently, initial expectations far exceed the realities of a teen's experience. For example, a Boomer owner of a yogurt shop recognized that "teenagers don't see the long haul, the fact that if you treat people well you'll get repeat business. They see it as a more immediate, one-time interaction. They don't see the Big Picture."

Helping young employees "see the Big Picture" is the job of management. So is holding them accountable for their actions. A Gen X manager in a Colorado video store confided, "I become ever more amazed each year by the attitude that younger employees bring with them. Many have very little respect for their job and responsibilities. Many do not accept any accountability for their actions on the job and how their actions affect other workers and customers."

It is also the job of management to support teens in developing a team-centered mindset. The Gen X Co-Coordinator of Youth Programs at a Boston museum observed, "I think for teenagers it is a big paradigm shift to realize that they are representing the museum, and that what they do reflects not just on themselves, but on the entire institution. Teenagers are still developing socially, and they are coming from an egotistical mindset. Their first job is the time for them to shift out of thinking only about 'me, me, me' and seeing themselves as part of a bigger team that is serving the public. What they do reflects not just on themselves, but on the entire institution."

To expect young workers to arrive at your workplace with the wisdom, expertise, and people-savvy that adults take years to learn is unrealistic and counterproductive. Expectations need to be tempered when new hires first walk in the door, and then accelerated as managers work with them every day. It's a fact: Like Boomers, Gen Yers thrive on challenge. They want the excitement of learning new things and stretching themselves. The initial challenges the workplace throws at them, then, need to build the confidence and competencies they'll need to soar. If their wings are tested and strengthened first, they'll fly even higher.

How Gen Y–Friendly Is Customer Service Training?

To discover the quality of customer service training Gen Yers were typically offered, we asked our Yers the following five questions:

1. Does the business you work for stress the importance of customer service? If so, how?

2. What kind of customer service training did you initially receive when you started your job?

3. What kind of ongoing training in customer service skills have you received?

4. What are the biggest challenges you face handling customers?

5. What suggestions would you have for managers who are trying to figure out how best to train young workers in customer service skills?

Typical of their generation, Yers were bluntly honest about how their managers were addressing—or failing to address—customer service training. Most of them understood that keeping customers happy is the key to a business's success. Most agreed that their employers conveyed their commitment to customer service in employee handbooks or in policy statements. Some applauded the training they initially receive, but admitted they've received no ongoing training. Others said they had to learn most of their service skills by the seat of their pants through trial and error. Many had practical insights into how managers could make ongoing customer service training more valuable for them.

Gen Yer Tips on Training

Among the many tips Yers offered managers on how to train them effectively, three stood out: role-plays, frequent tests, and games with prizes.

Role-Plays

While most adults cringe at the thought of this kind of training, Gen Yers consider practice a major confidence builder. They see role-playing real-life situations as a way to help them reflect on and think through encounters with difficult customers before they occur. However, not only do Yers want to learn what to do and say in challenging situations, they want to practice nonverbal skills as well.

As a server in an upscale restaurant advised us, "Tell managers not to assume we know listening skills, like letting a customer finish speaking before we start, or making eye contact while speaking, or how to be assertive without being offensive. We need practice." Give your Yers the practice they need.

Frequent Tests

The second Gen Y tip may also surprise older managers: Test us on what you want us to know. A 19-year-old retail sales associate says, "I believe an effective training program must be personal. Something the new employee can see and feel. A program that has steps, tests, passing scores, and rewards. The young person needs to be accountable for progress and successful completion of each step."

Holding employees accountable for their learning is a refreshing insight applicable to any generation. However, when it comes to Gen Y, it's an expectation. From pre-school through college, they're the most tested generation in history. So, the 17-year-old bank teller prides herself on taking post-training exams and meeting the high standards for a passing grade, and the 16-year-old movie theater cashier thinks pop quizzes on operating procedures are par for the course.

Games and Prizes

While customer service is a serious business, teens say the best managers don't present it seriously. Fun activities, customer service games, and great prizes light their fires and keep them motivated.

One teen reported that his retail store manager gives employees a smiley face on a game card whenever they're caught delivering great customer service. When the card is full, it's entered into a monthly drawing for prizes like a DVD player or TV. A second said her employer used secret shoppers to rate customer service performance. High scorers' names are put into a regional drawing. The prize: a new car. A third added that all high scorers in her business are rewarded with a full day off with pay. "That's like getting an A-plus in school," she smiled.

Engage Gen Yers in creating their own customer service games based on principles, standards, or skills they're presently learning. For example, if they're learning how to implement the "Always under-promise, over-deliver" principle, they can document and submit their weekly experiences into a drawing for a great prize. Or, if their current training is focused on problem-solving skills, they may role-play a situation they handled during the week at the next team meeting. The most effective performances are rewarded.

Also, ask Yers to identify the incentives that would propel them into action. Since Gen Y is a highly diverse cohort, expect rewards to be as varied as they are: gift certificates to restaurants or music stores; bigger discounts from the business; one-time cash bonuses; time off; entry into drawings for larger prizes. Whatever the game, ground rules or menu of rewards, Yers say they want opportunities to "learn and earn" as they develop into customer service experts.

The Shoddy Service Crisis: Where Are You?

It's no secret that businesses in every industry get low grades for their customer service practices. According to the Small Business Administration, 68 percent of dissatisfied customers won't return to a business because of the shoddy treatment they received from employees.

But you have a choice: Either continue to fuel the shoddy service crisis or become part of the solution. If you are willing to invest time, energy, and training in equipping your young Gen Yers with the essential skills of customer service, you will develop experts who will not only serve your customers today but also satisfy and surprise them tomorrow. That's an urgent long-term benefit worth your immediate attention.

Conclusion:
What You Need to Know
After You Read This Book

Here Come the New Gen Mixers

THE VICE-PRESIDENT of a large outplacement corporation confided in us: "After many changes in my career, I have learned to be more Gen X at 50 than anyone. You see, being raised by parents of the 1950s, I was told to find a good job, learn to type, and the rest will come. Leaving with the plaques and recognition after 30 years was supposed to be my goal. Well, it doesn't work that way. The way it works is to be up on the latest, be willing to change, be enthusiastic, articulate, and knowledgeable about technology. If you can't talk it, you won't be able to walk it!"

We couldn't have said it better! That's "the way it works" for people of every generation. The most successful people in the twenty-first century, then, will be true "Gen Mixers," people of all ages who bring to work their enthusiasm, talents, skills, expertise, wisdom, and voracious desire to learn and to teach. They may or may not have memories of World War II or Watergate. They may or may not have experienced command-and-control leadership or pay-your-dues ladder climbing. They may or may not have been latchkey kids or techno-whizzes. What they will be, however, is 100 percent responsible for how they create their lives, take care of themselves and their families, and use their experience to collaborate on getting the best work done every day. They will be the consummate free agents.

High Maintenance Is a Multigenerational Issue

How you manage these free agents—one person at a time, one day at a time—will take more time and skill than ever before. Whether you're creating flexible work arrangements for a new hire studying for an MBA, for a Gen X mom who wants to telecommute, for a Boomer who's exploring phased retirement, or for a retired Schwarzkopfer who's working as a project manager; whether you're setting goals and deadlines with each person on your team or offering them coaching-style feedback, just-in-time training, or leadership opportunities; whether you're trying to discover how to recognize and reward high performers on your team, management today is high-maintenance work.

Yes, Gen Y has gained the reputation for being the highest-maintenance workforce in history, and that's true. However, as the needs and expectations of each generation change during the Generational Shift, high maintenance will be a multigenerational issue. So, get ready to roll up your sleeves, get in there, and seize every opportunity you can to become a great Gen Mix manager. Your organization urgently needs you to succeed.

Recommended Resources

Multigenerational Resources

Foot, David K., and Daniel Stoffman. *Boom, Bust & Echo 2000: Profiting from the Demographic Shift in the New Millennium.* Toronto: Stoddart Publishing, 2000.

Karp, Hank, Connie Fuller, and Danilo Sirias. *Bridging the Boomer–Xer Gap: Creating Authentic Teams for High Performance at Work.* Palo Alto, CA: Davies-Black Publishing, 2002.

Lancaster, Lynne, and David Stillman. *When Generations Collide: Who They Are. Why They Clash. How to Solve the Generational Puzzle at Work.* New York: HarperCollins, 2002.

Strauss, William, and Neil Howe. *The Fourth Turning: What the Cycles of History Tell Us About America's Next Rendezvous with Destiny.* New York: Broadway Books, 1997.

Strauss, William, and Neil Howe. *Generations: The History of America's Future, 1584 to 2069.* New York: William Morrow & Co, 1992.

Zemke, Ron, Claire Raines, and Bob Filipczak. *Generations at Work: Managing the Clash of Veterans, Boomers, Xers, and Nexters in Your Workplace.* New York: AMACOM, 1999.

Schwarzkopfer and Boomer Resources

DeLong, David. *Lost Knowledge: Confronting the Threat of an Aging Workforce.* New York: Oxford University Press, 2004.

Dychtwald, Ken, and Daniel J. Kadlec. *The Power Years: A User's Guide to the Rest of Your Life.* New Jersey: John Wiley & Sons, Inc, 2005.

Goldberg, Beverly. *Age Works: What Corporate America Must Do to Survive the Graying of the Workforce.* New York: Free Press, 2000.

Moses, Susan. *Reinventing Aging: Baby Boomers and Civic Engagement.* Harvard School of Public Health/ MetLife Foundation, 2004. (Free report available online.)

Stone, Marika and Howard. *Too Young to Retire: 101 Ways to Start the Rest of Your Life.* New York: The Penguin Group, 2004.

For the latest trends and research on aging and retirement, see:

www.aarp.org
www.go60.com
www.kiplinger.com/planning/retirement
www.retirementliving.com
www.reinventingaging.com
www.wiredseniors.com
www.2young2retire.com

Generation X and Generation Y Resources

Chester, Eric. *Getting Them to Give A Damn: How to Get Your Front Line to Care About Your Bottom Line.* New York: Dearborn Publishing, 2005.

Draut, Tamara. *Strapped: Why America's 20- and 30-Somethings Can't Get Ahead.* New York: Doubleday, 2006.

Furman, Elina. *Boomerang Nation.* New York: Fireside Books, Simon & Schuster, Inc., 2005.

Howe, Neil, and William Strauss. *Millennials Rising: The Next Great Generation.* New York: Vintage Books, 2000.

Kamenetz, Anya. *Generation Debt: Why Now Is a Terrible Time To Be Young.* New York: Riverhead, 2006.

Wilner, Abby, and Cathy Stocker. *Quarterlife Crisis: The Unique Challenges of Life in Your Twenties.* New York: Tarcher/Putnam, 2001.

Wilner, Abby, and Cathy Stocker. *The Quarterlifer's Companion: How to Get On the Right Career Path, Control Your Finances, and Find the Support Network You Need to Thrive.* New York: McGraw-Hill, 2005.

Additional RainmakerThinking, Inc., Resources

Gibson, Donald, Ph.D., and Bruce Tulgan. *Managing Anger in the Workplace.* Amherst, MA: HRD Press, 2002.

Martin, Carolyn A., and Bruce Tulgan. *The Customer Service Intervention: Bottom Line Tactics for Front Line Managers.* Amherst, MA: HRD Press, 2003.

Martin, Carolyn A., and Bruce Tulgan. *Managing Generation Y: Global Citizens Born in the Late Seventies and Early Eighties.* Amherst, MA: HRD Press, 2001.

Sormaz, Heidi, Ph.D., and Bruce Tulgan. *Performance Under Pressure: Managing Stress in the Workplace.* Amherst, MA: HRD Press, 2003.

Tulgan, Bruce. *Career Skills for the New Economy.* Amherst, MA: HRD Press, 2000.

Tulgan, Bruce. *FAST Feedback®.* Second ed. Amherst, MA: HRD Press, 1999.

Tulgan, Bruce. *HOT Management.* Amherst, MA: HRD Press, 2004.

Tulgan, Bruce. *JUSTinTIME Leadership.* Amherst, MA: HRD Press, 2000.

Tulgan, Bruce. *The Manager's Pocket Guide to Generation X.* Amherst, MA: HRD Press, 1997.

Tulgan, Bruce. *Managing Generation X: How to Bring Out the Best in Young Talent.* Revised ed. New York: W.W. Norton, 2000. (First published Santa Monica, CA: Merritt, 1995.)

Tulgan, Bruce. *Recruiting the Workforce of the Future.* Second ed. Amherst, MA: HRD Press, 2000.

Tulgan, Bruce. *Winning the Talent Wars.* New York: W.W. Norton, 2001.

Tulgan, Bruce. *Work This Way.* New York: Hyperion, 1998.

Tulgan, Bruce, and Jeff Coombs. *Strategic Employee Polls.* Amherst, MA: HRD Press, 1998.